WHAT THE CRITICS SAY:

A very worthwhile addition to any travel library.
                                                    —WCBS Newsradio

Armed with these guides, you may never again stay in a conventional hotel.
                                                    —Travelore Report

Easily carried ... neatly organized ... wonderful. A helpful addition to my travel library. The authors wax as enthusiastically as I do about the almost too-quaint-to-believe Country Inns.
                                                    —San Francisco Chronicle

One can only welcome such guide books and wish them long, happy, and healthy lives in print.
                                                    —Wichita Kansas Eagle

This series of pocket-sized paperbacks will guide travelers to hundreds of little known and out of the way inns, lodges, and historic hotels.... a thorough menu.
                                                    —(House Beautiful's) Colonial Homes

Charming, extremely informative, clear and easy to read; excellent travelling companions.
                                                    —Books-Across-The-Sea *(The English Speaking Union)*

...a fine selection of inviting places to stay... provide excellent guidance....
                                                    —Blair & Ketchum's Country Journal

Obviously designed for our kind of travel.... [the authors] have our kind of taste.
                                                    —Daily Oklahoman

The first guidebook was so successful that they have now taken on the whole nation.... Inns are chosen for charm, architectural style, location, furnishings and history.
                                                    —Portland Oregonian

Very fine travel guides.
                                                    —Santa Ana (Calif.) Register

A wonderful source for planning trips.
                                                    —Northampton (Mass.) Gazette

Hundreds of lovely country inns reflecting the charm and hospitality of various areas.
                                                    —Youngstown (Ohio) Vindicator

Many quaint and comfy country inns... The authors have a grasp of history and legend.
                                                    —Dallas (Tx.) News

...pocketsize books full of facts.... attractively made and illustrated.
                                                    —New York Times Book Review

Some genius must have measured the average American dashboard, because the Compleat Traveler's Companions fit right between the tissues and bananas on our last trip.... These are good-looking books with good-looking photographs.... very useful.

                                                    —East Hampton (N.Y.) Star

ALSO AVAILABLE IN THE COMPLEAT TRAVELER SERIES

☐ Country Inns & Historic Hotels of Great Britain

☐ Country Inns & Historic Hotels of Canada

☐ Country Inns & Historic Hotels of Ireland

☐ Country New England Inns

☐ Country Inns & Historic Hotels of the Middle Atlantic States

☐ Country Inns & Historic Hotels of the South

☐ Country Inns & Historic Hotels of the Midwest & Rocky Mountain States

☐ Country Inns & Historic Hotels of the West & Southwest

☐ Country New England Historical & Sightseeing Guide

☐ Country New England Antiques, Crafts, & Factory Outlets

☐ Guide to California and the Pacific Northwest

☐ Guide to Texas and the Southwest

☐ Guide to the South

☐ *George Ferguson's* Europe by Eurail

☐ *George Ferguson's* Britain by Britrail

☐ The Total Traveler by Ship (*Ethel Blum*)

If your local bookseller, gift shop, or country inn does not stock a particular title, ask them to order directly from Burt Franklin & Co., Inc., 235 East 44th Street, New York, New York 10017, U.S.A. Telephone orders are accepted from recognized retailers and credit card holders. In the United States, call, toll free, 800-223-0766 during regular business hours. (In New York State, call 212-687-5250.)

COUNTRY INNS

Lodges, and Historic Hotels of

Canada

by

Anthony Hitchcock

and

Jean Lindgren

BURT FRANKLIN & CO.

Published by Burt Franklin & Company
235 East Forty-fourth Street
New York, New York 10017

© 1980 by Burt Franklin & Co., Inc.
All rights reserved

Library of Congress Cataloging in Publication Data

Hitchcock, Anthony
Country inns, lodges, and historic hotels
of Canada.
(The Compleat traveler's companion).
Includes index.
1. Hotels, taverns, etc.—Canada—Directories.
I. Lindgren, Jean, joint author.   II. Title.   III. Series.

ISBN 0–89102–186–8
ISBN 0–89102–161–2 pbk.

1 3 4 2

Manufactured in the United States of America

Contents

Introduction

CANADA IS THE second largest country in the world. It is no small wonder, then, that her ten provinces offer an extraordinary range of natural vistas from the Atlantic coast of her Maritimes to the Laurentian Mountains, across the prairies of the central provinces, over the Canadian Rockies, and out to the Pacific shore. Much of Canada's history has been preserved in its architecture. Many buildings, in Quebec Province, for example, predate 1700.

Although there is mounting evidence that Canada's Eastern Seaboard was visited by early Viking expeditions, its first recorded exploration was that of the Gulf of Saint Lawrence by Jacques Cartier in 1534. Early settlement of the eastern regions of the country was by French settlers, and even today French-speaking citizens account for more than a quarter of the population of this bilingual country. British expansion in the New World resulted in Anglo-French conflicts that ended in 1763 with the establishment of British rule over all of the settled regions, including the portions previously known as New France. Not long after that, the French-speaking people of Quebec were given rights to use their own language and practice their religion. The country became united as the Dominion of Canada on July 1, 1867, after promulgation of the British North America Act.

In the pages that follow, you will discover a wide range of inns, lodges, and historic hotels that span the continent, although the greatest concentration is in the eastern and western provinces. It is the purpose of this book to describe as accurately as possible a variety of accommodations that offer history, romance, charm and that are alternatives to the standard motel rooms that blanket Canada as thoroughly as the United States to the south. We have deliberately not introduced a rating system, because no single system could possibly encompass the wide range of accommodations—from small guest houses to grand historic hotels—that we have included.

Once you have selected possible inns for your visit, we suggest that you write for additional descriptive information from the innkeepers.

Read the brochures, look at the pictures, check the maps, and determine if the inns will actually meet your needs. Each is likely to have special qualities that can enhance one's personal pleasure. Do not hesitate to discuss your needs with innkeepers. We find them to be sensitive to the needs of their guests and happy to describe their inns.

We have quoted the most recent room rates in a combined rate chart and index at the end of the book. Readers should note that the listed rates are *subject to change*. While the quoted rates are for double occupancy in most cases, single travelers as well as larger groups should inquire about special rates. We list daily room rates as based on the American Plan (AP, all three meals included), Modified American Plan (MAP, breakfast and dinner included), or European Plan (EP, no meals or a light Continental breakfast only). In many cases a tax and a service charge will be added. Be sure to ask. Children and pets present special problems for many inns. If either is *not* welcome at an inn it is noted in the description. These regulations also often change, and it is imperative that families traveling with either inquire in advance. Even though many inns state they are open all year, we find that many close during slow periods. Call first to confirm your room reservations.

When we first planned our trip to Quebec we wondered if our very limited knowledge of the language would be a detriment in the areas where little English is written or spoken. We were relieved to discover that our efforts to speak the language were warmly greeted, and often residents of the province would answer us in English once we made an attempt to communicate in French. It is worth the trouble to learn a few basic phrases and to carry a dictionary to help one to decipher restaurant menus.

We suggest that before traveling to any province you write to its department of travel and tourism. Ask for the provincial road map and a packet of general travel information. If you have special travel interests or needs, the department can often send special pamphlets or hints. In the pages that follow, readers will discover that the material is organized by province. Within each province, listings are alphabetical by the names of the towns and villages. For those seeking a particular inn, there is an index at the end of the book, which also contains rate and credit-card information.

The inns described in this book were chosen for their inherent charm, based partially on their architectural style, location, furnishings, and history. The information incorporated here came from several sources: our personal knowledge of inns, recommendations by people we deem reliable, and our own surveys of innkeepers. We have made every effort to provide information as carefully and accurately as possible, but we remind readers that all information, especially that on rates, is subject to change. We hope this book will grow in usefulness in succeeding editions, and we would be grateful for suggestions and comments from our readers. We will make every effort to answer all letters personally. Please write to us in care of our publishers: Burt Franklin & Co., 235 East Forty-fourth Street, New York, NY 10017.

Have a good trip!

JEAN LINDGREN
ANTHONY HITCHCOCK

SOURCES OF USEFUL TRAVEL INFORMATION

Travel Alberta
10065 Jasper Avenue
Edmonton, AL, Canada T5J OH4
403-427-4321

Tourism British Columbia
1117 Wharf Street
Victoria, BC, Canada V8W 2Z2
604-387-1642

Manitoba Department of Tourism
200 Vaughn Street
Winnipeg, MB, Canada R3C 1T5
204-946-7421

Tourism New Brunswick
P.O. Box 12345
Fredericton, NB, Canada E3B 5C3
506-453-2377

Newfoundland and Labrador
Tourist Services Division
Confederation Building
Saint John's NF Canada A1A 2Y3
709-737-2830

Nova Scotia Department of Tourism
Travel Division
P.O. Box 130
Halifax, NS, Canada B3J 2R5

Ontario Travel
Queen's Park
Toronto, ON, Canada M7A 2E5
416-965-4008

PEI Tourism Services
P.O. Box 940
Charlottetown, PEI, Canada
C1A 7M5
902-892-2457

Quebec Tourism
C.P. 20,000
Quebec, Canada G1K 7X2
418-643-3127

Saskatchewan Travel
1825 Lorne Street
Regina, SK, Canada S4P 3N1
306-565-2300

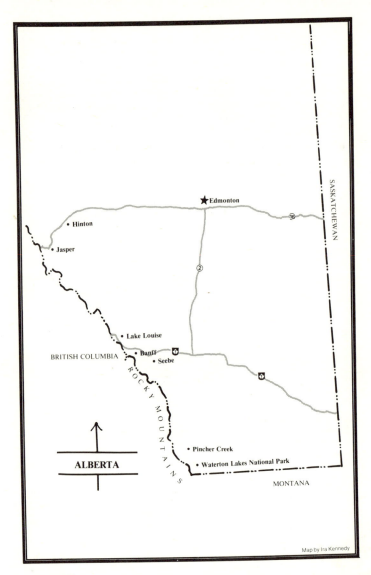

ALBERTA

Map by Ira Kennedy

Alberta

BANFF SPRINGS HOTEL

Spray Avenue, Banff, Alberta. Mailing address: P.O. Box 960, Banff, Alberta TOL OEO, Canada. 403-762-2211. *Innkeeper:* Canadian Pacific Hotels. Open all year.

Sir William Van Horne, vice-president of the Canadian Pacific Railway at the turn of the century, used to quip, "Since we can't export the scenery, we shall have to import the tourists." Probably no other hotel in the Canadian Pacific chain has quite such a firm claim on impossible-to-export scenery. The Banff Springs Hotel is an 1887 baronial edifice rising almost a dozen stories above the surrounding firs in the heart of the Canadian Rockies. Overlooking a bend in the Bow River, it is a full-service, first-class hotel. Its lobby has a fireplace more than 6 feet wide that is surrounded by polished marble floors and arches leading to some of the many shops and dining rooms. The baronial theme is carried out in much of the hotel with heavy beams, rich carpeting, antique wooden furniture, and large chandeliers.

The Banff Springs is now open all year thanks to the recent development of the surrounding ski areas. Winter offerings include a busy après-ski lounge and ski fashion shows and films. Steaming mugs of hot buttered rum and gluwein are served to warm the throngs of skiers who populate the hotel from the first flakes of snow onward. There is a heated indoor Olympic-size swimming pool surrounded by a two-story gallery. Guests come to the hotel in summer for its pollen-free air, the par seventy-one eighteen-hole golf course, tennis on five courts, horseback riding, and other activities of a major resort. The decor of the hotel's public rooms is carried into its guest rooms, some of which have romantic touches like ceiling canopies over the beds. Many rooms have color television.

There are five restaurants to choose from within the hotel. The Alberta and Alhambra rooms both feature a selection of meals

ranging from turkey or duck to fish and steak. The Rob Roy Supper Club offers steaks, roast beef, and fish and a dance band during supper. The Potpourri downstairs is a gourmet dining room featuring fondues and Japanese foods. The Café Espresso coffeehouse offers a selection of coffees and espresso and Danish pastries and other sweets.

Accommodations: 527 rooms with private bath. *Driving Instructions:* The hotel is reached by Route 1 from Calgary.

Hinton

BLACK CAT GUEST RANCH

Brule Road, Hinton, Alberta. Mailing address: P.O. Box 542, Hinton, Alberta TOE 1BO, Canada. 403-866-2107. *Innkeepers:* Jerry and Mary Bond. Open all year.

Black Cat Guest Ranch, a sprawling modern complex on the eastern boundary of Jasper National Park, has been taking in guests since its beginnings in 1935. The Bonds built the present lodge in 1976 using only local unpainted woods and its lines are clean and attractive against the backdrop of the mountains. The scenic wilderness and the front range of the Canadian Rockies can be seen from the verandas and picture windows of the lodge's southern face. Many artists and photographers are attracted by the natural beauty of the region. Rolling pastures and woodland are the ranch's immediate surroundings.

The guest rooms, which open onto long porches overlooking the nearby Rockies, have picture windows that provide indoor mountain views. They are in two wings branching off from the central house with its high ceilings and 1,800-square-foot living room. In this popular gathering spot, the Bonds have created a homelike setting with comfortable couches and chairs, a library, game tables, and a piano. The centerpiece is the big stone fireplace that has a curly-horned ram's head peering down from above its mantel. The room's paneled walls are decorated with mounted trophy heads and hides, and a large open balcony and rough-log staircase overlook it. Everyone gathers in the adjoining dining room for a family-style meal. Mary Bond cooks a big dinner with one entree that changes daily. There are usually homemade soups, roasts, chops, barbecued meats, or perhaps a hearty Italian meal. Desserts and biscuits are homemade, and for in-season treats the menu has wild raspberries or local wild mushrooms. Guests are invited to bring their own liquor if they wish to have a drink. The Bonds provide bar facilities in the dining room.

In summer the ranch offers scenic tours into Jasper and to the nearby Columbia Icefield. There are canoe trips and four-wheel-drive adventures into the wilderness area. Horseback riding is available at the ranch, and there is a children's riding camp on the property in summer. In winter the place comes alive with cross-country skiers and snowmobilers traversing the many miles of trails, including several set trails for skiers and hundreds of miles of old logging trails for both skiers and snowmobilers.

Accommodations: 16 rooms with private bath. *Pets:* Not permitted. *Driving Instructions:* Turn north off Route 16 at Grande Cache Junction, west of Hinton. Go about 4 miles over the Athabasca River bridge and up a hill to Brule Road. Turn left and go 9 miles to the ranch sign. The ranch is also known as the PB Ranch.

Jasper

JASPER PARK LODGE

Jasper, Alberta TOE 1EO, Canada. 403-852-3301. *Innkeeper:* Canadian National Hotels. Open mid-April through October.

Jasper Park Lodge, a large, full-service luxury resort, is encircled by Jasper Park and the ice-capped peaks of the Canadian Rockies. The lodge building and its complex of functional, attractive guest cabins are in a sheltered setting of manicured lawns and gardens, golf courses, and tall, dark pines. Most of the cottages and the lodge itself overlook the clear mountain lake, Lac Beauport, which offers a double image of the unique scenery.

The original main lodge was built in 1923 by the Canadian National Railroad, which still provides transportation up to the resort from the railroad station in Jasper. The old lodge, said to be the largest single-story log structure in the world, burned to the ground in 1952. All through that winter four hundred workers labored to complete the new building for a "spring thaw" reopening in 1953. The new structure, of fieldstone and reinforced concrete, has large expanses of picture windows. Jasper Park Lodge today blends with and complements the surrounding wilderness. The entrance to the main building is flanked by two 9-foot-high totem poles. In the heart of its lobby is a stone fireplace (actually two fireplaces back to back) rising 33 feet to the roof and with hearth openings 7 feet wide. The lobby is divided into many lounging areas, some with lake and mountain views, others a little more intimate. A wide stone terrace outside the lobby overlooks the lake and has access to an adjacent glassed-in cocktail lounge. The main dining room, which can seat about 550 people at one time, has one whole wall and a west gable of glass with views of the lake. The lodge prides itself on a wide selection of cuisines served in four separate dining rooms. The Beauvert Room specializes in Continental food; the Moose's Nook features a Canadian menu; steaks are the specialty of Henry House; and the Tonquin Room has a seven-course meal.

In the late 1950s and early 1960s most of the original log cabins accommodating guests were replaced with modern cedar chalets. The nine remaining log cabins are in great demand by those in the know. The new chalets vary in size and layout; they can have from two to thirty bedrooms and all have individually controlled heat. Most rooms have either a furnished patio or a balcony. The guest rooms in the main building, mostly reserved for handicapped people, can be reached by elevator and have a rooftop garden.

There are almost unlimited recreational and sightseeing possibilities here. A new swimming pool is near a health spa with saunas, steam baths, whirlpools, and an exercise room. Horseback trail-riding is provided at the new stables, and golfing is excellent on the lodge's course. Jasper Park provides scores of activities from tame nature walks or drives to mountain climbing and white-water canoeing. Among its many other offerings are snowmobile tours and the Jasper Sky Tram; pack trips; scuba diving in clear mountain lakes; and wildlife stalking for photographers. The park and its surrounds are home to many wild creatures, such as coyotes, moose, bighorn sheep, and bears. The Jasper Park Lodge will provide guests with all the area literature and information.

Accommodations: 365 rooms with private bath. *Driving Instructions:* The lodge is 4 miles from the town of Jasper, off Route 16.

Lake Louise

CHATEAU LAKE LOUISE

Lake Louise, Alberta TOL 050, Canada. 403-522-3511. *Innkeeper:* Canadian Pacific Hotels (Michael Broadhurst, Manager). Open in 1980 May 22 through October 12.

Chateau Lake Louise is a sedate Victorian edifice in the midst of Banff National Park. The "jewel of the Canadian Rockies," a fairyland castle-like structure on the shores of jade-green Lake Louise high in the mountains, is at an altitude of 6,000 feet, between the lake and a large glacier. Its grounds include gardens and flower-lined paths and a large swimming pool area, all surrounded by dark pines against the purples and blues of mountains, glacier, and deep valleys. Many resort activities are available, such as hiking on groomed trails, horseback riding, fishing, and canoeing. The Canadian Pacific Company has been working winters toward opening the hotel as a year-round resort with welcoming log fires in its many stone hearths. Just outside the door is the Lake Louise Ski Area with its highest point at 7,800 feet, a vertical drop of 2,600 feet, and a run of 5 miles. The ski patrol maintains more than 35 miles of cross-country ski trails. Snowshoeing, ice skating, sleigh rides, and toboggan rides are all here at the Chateau's doorstep.

The very first chateau was built in 1890, and there has been one on this spot ever since. In the early part of the twentieth-century a wooden section occasionally burned and would be rebuilt and a wing or two would be added, until the hotel took its present form in 1925.

Guest lodgings vary from "standard" rooms with views of the lake or mountains to "superior" and "deluxe" suites with living rooms and one or two bedrooms. All accommodations are furnished with comfortable, traditional hotel furniture and carpets. Lakeview rooms and suites are in much demand; the hotel cannot guarantee to fill all requests for these rooms but do take them into consideration. One of the main reasons for their great popularity is the view of the sunrise over Lake Louise, a spectacle that has been voted one of the "ten greatest scenic sights" by travel editor Frederick Babcock of the *Chicago Daily Tribune.*

In keeping with its size the hotel offers guests and the public a number of dining choices. Breakfasts and lunches are served buffet-style, and the dining rooms and cocktail lounges offer a variety of menus. The Victorian Room and the Fairview Supper Club are most popular for elegant evening dinners. The Red Room, a cocktail lounge with a large stone hearth, has dancing every weekday afternoon and the special attraction of vistas of the nearby glacier from its picture windows. For a bird's-eye view of the Chateau and its environs, visitors should be sure to take the gondola trip to the top of the glacier; it is quite an experience.

Accommodations: 373 rooms with private bath. *Driving Instructions:* Chateau Lake Louise is within Banff National Park, about 38 miles west of Banff on the Trans-Canada Highway.

GLADSTONE MOUNTAIN GUEST RANCH

Route 507, Pincher Creek, Alberta. Mailing address: P. O. Box 1286, Pincher Creek, Alberta TOK 1WO, Canada. *Innkeepers:* Charles and Valerie Ridder. Open all year.

In 1935 local oil millionaires Cross and Boyd built five small log cabins and a log "Cook House," which were then operated as the J.O. Guest Ranch. When Chuck and Val Ridder bought the ranch in 1977, it had not been operated for more than fifteen years. Undeterred, they set out to restore the original buildings to meet current standards, and they added to the old buildings to provide for more guests. Fortunately, the Ridders have 300 of their 600 acres covered with trees and thus had access to ample logs for all new construction. And—unlike in the old days—the Ridders could use modern transportation to bring the felled trees to the ranch site. In the 1930s the logs were skidded out of the woods by horses during the winter, when they would slide more easily over the snow. Chuck and Val barked every log by hand, and then Chuck proceeded to construct the new buildings.

Probably the most important additions were the new dining rooms with their log walls, exposed-pole roof rafters, stone fireplace, and wagon-wheel hurricane-lamp chandeliers. The Gladstone's ranch-style meals frequently include chicken and dumplings, steak, beef pie, rainbow trout, lobster, or a Gladstone specialty—North American buffalo steak. Homebaked breads, bannock, and apple pie and other homecooked desserts accompany the meals. The beef is raised on the ranch and the honey comes direct from one of the Ridders' hives. Breakfast is served in the renovated Cook House, now stripped of many coats of blue paint to reveal its original log walls.

Guest may stay in the five original log cabins that share a public washhouse (showers, flush toilets, and a recently added sauna) or in one of the four new cabins built by Chuck. The latter have private bathrooms with showers. All the cabins are on a hillside overlooking the mountains, a leisurely half-hour's walk away.

The Ridders have maintained the original "dude ranch" atmosphere at their working ranch. Their south fence borders a national forest reserve, providing guests with unlimited hiking and skiing trails. The many ranch activities include riding and even herding cattle and branding, for the more adventurous. But most guests come for the open space and clean air. There are no television sets, no phones, no radio, and no tennis; swimming is done in a ranch pond fed by cool mountain streams. Scenic trails fan out from the ranch, and guides lead guests on trail rides through flowering alpine meadows and thick forests all summer long. There are hayrides, barbecues, hiking, and (in winter) skiing and showshoeing. Hunters are welcome; most come for black bear, elk, sheep, and mule and whitetail deer. If you come, bring your camera—photography is fine in any season.

Accommodations: 9 cabins, 4 with private bath. *Pets:* Not permitted. *Driving Instructions:* From Calgary, take Route 2 south to Fort Macleod, then take Route 3 southwest to Pincher Creek. The ranch is 17 miles west of Pincher Creek on Route 507.

S COWLEY

Seebe

RAFTER SIX GUEST RANCH (KANANASKIS INN)

Seebe, Alberta. Mailing address: Seebe, Alberta TOL 1X0, Canada. 403-673-3622. *Innkeepers:* Stan and Gloria Cowley. Open all year.

The name Rafter Six comes from the early brand (a half-diamond over the number 6) assigned to Colonel Walker of the North-West Mounted Police. Walker had come to Alberta in the late nineteenth century to start the first commercial logging enterprise in the province. In 1929 the ranch was turned into a guest operation by Eva and Alvin Guinn, and over the years it has grown to be one of the largest log-structure complexes in North America, with a rustic main lodge and smaller overnight log cabins. In 1954 it was a location for the Marilyn Monroe movie *River of No Return* and it has since been used for many Walt Disney productions and for the filming of *Grizzly Adams, The Wilderness Family,* and *Across the Great Divide*, as well as a number of television commercials.

The main lodge contains the dining room in what was the original log building, a cocktail lounge displaying a collection of animal skins, and a handicraft store featuring Indian leatherwork and beadwork.

Also in the main lodge are a sitting room for guests, a game room with pool, shuffleboard, and Ping-pong, and guest rooms with exposed-log walls, comfortable furniture, and original paintings. Guests who prefer more secluded accommodations are placed in one of the log cabins on the property.

Early on summer mornings, guests are greeted by the aromas of the Rafter Six Chuckwagon Breakfast of bacon, pancakes, and freshly brewed coffee. Moderately priced lunches offer a sandwich selection, soup, cold plates, and home-baked pies. For dinner, guests may choose from a menu including Rocky Mountain trout, steak, pork chops, and barbecued ribs. A Sunday smorgasbord often includes exotic dishes like roast buffalo.

Because Rafter Six is a guest ranch riding is an important activity. Trail rides are available on an hourly or a daily basis, and there are also hayrides and stagecoach rides. Rafter Six has begun to offer Western weddings in their outdoor chapel, with the ceremonies presided over by a local Indian chief in traditional costume. A heated swimming pool operates in summer, and most evenings have a campfire where guests can toast marshmallows and sing songs of the old West.

In winter the ranch offers cross-country skiing, skating, tobogganing, and sleigh riding on the ranch property. It is about thirty miles from Banff and 40 miles from Calgary, affording guests the opportunity to enjoy the larger towns' recreational and historical offerings.

Accommodations: 19 rooms in the lodge, plus 7 cabins. *Pets:* Not permitted. *Driving Instructions:* Take the Trans-Canada Highway 42 miles west of Calgary to the Rafter Six Ranch exit. The ranch is a mile south of the highway.

Waterton Lakes National Park

PRINCE OF WALES HOTEL

Waterton Lakes National Park, Alberta, Canada. Mailing Address: Glacier Park Co., East Glacier Park, MT 59434. (Off season: Glacier Park Co., 1735 East Fort Lowell, Suite 7, Tucson, AZ 85719.) 403-859-2231. (Off season: 602-795-0377 in Tucson.) *Innkeeper:* Don Hummel and the Glacier Park Co. Open early June through mid-September.

Waterton Lakes National Park is continuous with Montana's Glacier Park to the south and the two together form the Waterton-Glacier International Peace Park. This large continuous parkland and wilderness has always been a fine symbol to us of the friendship between the two great North American nations. The mountains surrounding Waterton Lake rise abruptly from the lakeshore and, because of their deposits of ore, reflect hues of gold, red, and purple. The motor launch *International* goes the length of the lake to Goat Haunt, Montana, where the U.S. Department of the Interior has a small museum.

Unlike the historic hotels on the American side of the border, the Prince of Wales, instead of having grown sideways with annexes, is still the tall, six-storied building that was constructed in 1926 and 1927 by the Great Northern Railway. It is on a hilltop above the township of Waterton, overlooking Waterton Lake, an international body of water that stretches more than 7 miles southward. On three sides are mountains that still bear the scars of successions of glaciers.

Lumber for the building (primarily fir and pine) was felled in Montana and processed at a sawmill and drying kiln on site in Canada. Many of the logs were hand-hewn, and the quality of the workmanship is apparent in both the lobby and the dining room. Because of severe winter winds the building was anchored to its site by means of large cables installed from its loft, through the structure, and into the ground itself.

The hotel has steep sloping roofs, balconies for most rooms, and fine views in all directions. The view from the lobby is past the township and lake into the U.S. Rockies. Each evening a trio plays chamber music in the lobby. There are many lake and lakeside activities including hiking, cruises, and horseback riding. Wildlife often approach the hotel and the township, where goats, sheep, and deer are frequently seen in the streets and gardens and on the hillsides. Most of the guest rooms have paneled walls; many on the lakeside have their own balconies. The menu at the Prince of Wales varies from year to year, but typical dinner meals start with relish boats and a choice of soup or juice. Entrees might include such items as mountain trout amandine, lamb chops, duckling à l'orange, and a choice of steaks. Some entrees reflect the hotel's British heritage; Yorkshire pudding is always served with the roast beef.

The Prince of Wales is one of four historic hotels in the International Peace Park. The others—Glacier Park Lodge, Many Glacier Hotel, and Lake MacDonald Lodge—are on the Montana side of the border and are described in our book *Country Inns, Lodges, and Historic Hotels of the Midwest and Rocky Mountain States*. For information about all lodging in the park, write to the Glacier Park Co. at the address above.

Accommodations: 82 rooms. *Pets:* Permitted if leashed. *Driving Instructions:* Take Route 5 to Waterton Lakes in the National Park.

British Columbia

AGUILAR HOUSE RESORT

Bamfield, British Columbia VOR 1BO, Canada. 604-728-3323.
Innkeepers: Florence and Bob Peel. Open Easter through
Canadian Thanksgiving (October).

Bamfield, a remote fishing village on the west coast of Vancouver
Island, is situated on both sides of a small inlet. Boats of every shape
and size are the prime mode of travel here. The town's Main Street is a
boardwalk connecting the houses and businesses along the waterfront. Nearby, in a parklike setting, is Aguilar House, which faces
Barkley Sound and the Pacific Ocean from its rugged coastal perch.
The innkeepers have spent a great deal of time and energy renovating
the secluded inn. It was built as a private home in 1932, and the Peels
bought it as an inn in 1971. They work very hard to assure guests of a
relaxing vacation. Both are knowledgeable about Bamfield's environs, history, tourist attractions, and residents. They share this enthusiastically and also provide an extensive library on local and natural
history. A favorite gathering spot is the lounge–living room, which
features an unusual brick-and-stone fireplace flanked by two large
picture windows. The sun setting over the Sound is a memorable view
from the room. No television or newspaper intrudes upon the ''out of
this world'' atmosphere of Aguilar and the town.

Guests may stay in either the main house or Augilar Cottage, a
housekeeping unit next door. (Aguilar, Anglicized from the Spanish
word for ''eagle,'' is named to honor the many eagles that nest

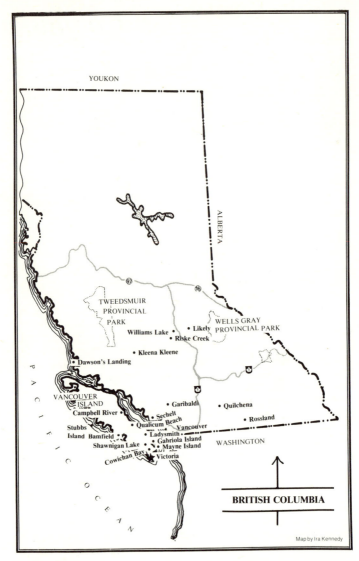

YOUKON

ALBERTA

97

16

TWEEDSMUIR
PROVINCIAL
PARK

WELLS GRAY
PROVINCIAL PARK

Williams Lake • • Likely

• Riske Creek

• Kleena Kleene

• Dawson's Landing

P
A
C
I
F
I
C

VANCOUVER
ISLAND

Campbell River

Stubbs
Island Bamfield

Shawnigan Lake

Cowichan Bay

• Garibaldi

• Sechelt

• Qualicum Beach

Vancouver

• Ladysmith

Gabriola Island

• Mayne Island

★ Victoria

• Quilchena

• Rossland

WASHINGTON

O
C
E
A
N

BRITISH COLUMBIA

Map by Ira Kennedy

around the inn and Barkley Sound.) The inn's bedrooms are sunny and modestly furnished and have "en suite" plumbing. In the dining room, another favorite rendezvous for guests and the Peels, meals are served family-style around a large table. They are hearty affairs with plenty of home-baked bread. The dinner of fresh spring salmon in season is not to be missed. Bob Peel has constructed a topographical map of the Sound that fills an entire wall of the room. It is a handy reference and spur to lively table conversation.

The setting at Aguilar is like a dream come true for lovers of seclusion. Walking trails entice one to explore the driftwood-strewn beaches and rocky headlands as well as the nearby rain forest. Visitors should be sure to bring along good hiking shores and rain gear for these excursions. The Peels' neighbors are of the Mootka Tribe, noted for their beautiful weavings of swamp-grass and cedar-bark baskets. Many activities occupy the days here, including fishing, boating, hiking, and scuba diving. One of the nicest pastimes is just to sit lazily out on the lawn, surrounded by hills with their dark, piney woods, and gaze out at the surf washing against lichen-covered rocks dotting the coastline.

Accommodations: 4 rooms sharing bath and 1 housekeeping unit. *Pets:* Only in Aguilar Cottage. *Driving Instructions:* The best way to get to the area is to leave your car in Port Alberni and take *M.V. Lady Rose* from there to Bamfield, a scenic three- to four-hour cruise. The boat leaves port at 8 A.M. on Monday, Tuesday, and Sunday. Float planes from Port Alberni make daily runs to Bamfield. There are 60 miles of industrial logging roads from Port Alberni to Bamfield for the adventurous, or one can boat down the inlet.

PAINTER'S LODGE AND FISHING RESORT

P.O. Box 460, 1625 McDonald Road, Campbell River, British Columbia V9W 5C1, Canada. 604-286-6201 or 604-286-6202. *Innkeeper:* T. A. T. Properties (Manager: Bryon Armstrong). Open all year.

Painter's Lodge is a salmon-fishing resort that attracts many personalities from stage, screen, and politics to some of the best sport fishing in the West. In a secluded spot overlooking the Strait of Georgia from the northwest corner of Vancouver Island, the lodge is rightfully called "world famous," because its guests come from all over the globe. In her book *Diamond in the Rough: The Campbell River Story*, author Helen Mitchell says: "The best-known and oldest of the local resorts which cater to tyee fishermen is Painters."

The lodge opened in 1938 and is going strong today. There is an Old World ambience despite the modern improvements and amenities. The fireside sitting room has a stone fireplace that is active on wintery days and cool evenings all year. Furnishings throughout the lodge are a blend of overstuffed chairs and couches and many antiques that add accents of interest. The walls are paneled and the chairs are next to burled end tables. The lounge is a friendly spot to gather for a cocktail in the evening, and the dining room adjacent has views of the ocean. From the lodge one may glimpse passenger liners silently passing in the blue dusk with lights glowing from decks and portholes. The menus at Painter's lean to prime ribs, steaks and mushrooms, and chops. The house specialty is the Captain's Plate of salmon, scallops, and oysters. Barbecues will be set up on request. After-dinner drinks are served in the newly remodeled and enlarged Sandbar Lounge with its mirrors, stained-glass windows, and copper-hooded fireplace. Guest rooms, comfortably furnished in traditional lodge decor, are in the lodge and in nearby cabins on the landscaped grounds.

The lounge lobby is filled from floor to ceiling with photos of movie stars, politicians, and world figures as well as "regular folks" who have something special in common; they are all members of the exclusive Tyee Club. All one has to do to become a member is land a fighting Pacific salmon that weighs in at more than 30 pounds. Painter's offers full fishing facilities year round; the big tyee run is in

July and August. The rest of the months are devoted to fishing (in season) for steelheads, Northern Coho, bluebacks, and rainbow trout. Lodge personnel not only take you out in 16-foot boats but wrap, box, freeze, smoke, or can your catch.

When guests are not fishing, and for the occasional non-fisherman, there are a multitude of recreational and sightseeing opportunities. At the lodge the heated outdoor swimming pool awaits, and golf and horseback riding are nearby. The government park at Elk Falls has scenic drives through stands of cedar and fir. A short ferry-cruise away is Quadra Island. The Indian Village and lighthouse at Cape Mudge are fine for sightseeing, and the area abounds with deserted beaches perfect for exploring and hiking.

Accommodations: 18 lodge rooms and 21 cabins; 4 share baths and the rest have showers or tub bathrooms. *Pets:* Not permitted. *Driving Instructions:* From Nanaimo on the eastern side of Vancouver Island, take Route 19 north to Campbell River. Proceed about 4 miles north of town on Route 9 to the lodge.

Cowichan Bay

WILCUMA LODGE AND RESORT

Lanes Road, Cowichan Bay, Vancouver Island, British Columbia. Mailing address: R. R. 3, Cobble Hill, British Columbia VOR 1LO, Canada. 604-748-8737. *Innkeeper:* Trev Pollard. Open all year.

Wilcuma Lodge, on Vancouver Island, is a three-story Tudor-style building dating from 1902. It forms the core of a small family resort and overlooks Cowichan Bay. Its public rooms combine some antique pieces with comfortable furniture of more recent vintage. High ceilings and freshly painted walls contrast with the dark beams and window trim of many of the rooms. There is wall-to-wall carpeting throughout much of the lodge, with an occasional Oriental rug before one of the several fireplaces. Some lodge guest rooms have antique furnishings, another has a fireplace in its own niche and a private bath. Set on a hill sloping gently to the sea, the lodge is surrounded by fir trees, flowering dogwood, and arbutus. To one side is a 60-foot heated freshwater swimming pool (although many guests prefer to take a dip along the coastline in front of the lodge). In addition to the lodge rooms, there are several more contemporary and some older

housekeeping cottages with paneled walls, wall-to-wall carpeting, and porches overlooking the sea. A dock leads from the shore to several boats that are always moored there. The bay is known to give up near-record catches of Chinook and Coho salmon throughout most of the season. There is also good fishing for brown, cutthroat, Dolly Varden, and rainbow trout in the nearby lakes and rivers.

Breakfast and dinner are offered to guests; the public is welcome to dine at the lodge in the evening. Dinner is served from an à la carte menu with starters like clam chowder, French onion soup (a house specialty), and escargots. Entrees are split between seafood dishes, such as King crab legs and fantail shrimp, and grilled steaks. For dessert there are pies, éclairs, fresh fruit, and ice cream.

Guests who wish to venture from the lodge should drive up to Duncan and the Forest Museum. Its grounds offer complete displays of old-time logging practices as well as rides on an old-fashioned steam train. Before starting out, you might also like to ask directions to the nearby House of Glass, made entirely out of old bottles. Recreation-minded guests often use the nearby grass tennis courts, among the oldest in the province, and play golf at the nearby nine-hole golf course.

Accommodations: 4 lodge guest rooms with private bath; 10 cottages with bath or shower. *Pets:* Permitted, but on a limited basis and with a charge. *Driving Instructions:* Take the Island Highway (Route 1) north from Victoria to Cowichan Bay Road (north of Mill Bay). Follow the signs to Wilcuma Resort.

RIVER'S LODGE

River's Inlet, Dawson's Landing, British Columbia VON 1MO, Canada. 604-685-2127. *Innkeepers:* Pat and George Ardley. Open all year.

River's Lodge is Canada's answer to Shangri-la. Near the mouth of River's Inlet, an area renowned for its fine fishing, the lodge is accessible primarily by seaplane from Vancouver some 250 miles to the south. River's Lodge was created as a salmon-fishing resort where guests could simultaneously experience life by the sea and in a wilderness area. Pat and George Ardley carried out this idea by renovating loggers' and trappers' cabins and setting them on rafts made of large logs that are securely tied to shore. The lodge floats on a sheltered bay where mirror-like waters reflect the mountains, dark pines, and moss-covered rocks at the shore. The lodge rides up and down with the tide, and its carpeted rooms overlook the water from multi-paned windows reaching from floor to ceiling. The red-painted wooden buildings with their white trim are connected by wooden walkways that also float on logs. Porches are decked out with a tub or two of flowers and the ever-present fish-weighing scales.

This is the Ardleys' permanent home, and guests are pampered as special friends. The guest rooms have down comforters piled high on the beds. Some of the walls in the lodge are painted in earth tones complementing the cedar paneling in the others. The inviting lounge–dining area has comfortable contemporary rocking chairs, upholstered chairs, and couches grouped around the fireplace where fires burn on cold mornings and chilly evenings. After dinner, guests sit by the hearth, sip hot chocolate and swap the day's adventure stories. The lodge provides ice and setups for guests who bring their own liquor, which may be obtained at a liquor store in the town of River's Inlet. It is also the place where guests can get their fishing licenses for a nominal fee. Because this is such a remote area, the Ardleys must provide their own electricity. A diesel generator is run only long enough to keep the freezers frozen, 12-volt battery lights keep the lodge lit in the evenings.

Meals and everything else here are made even better by the fresh sea air. Everything is cooked on the wood-burning stove, including

such delicacies as fresh fish with bearnaise sauce and chicken Kiev. Among the local seafoods available are crabs, prawns, abalone, salmon, clams, cod, and more. Meals come with freshly baked breads and rolls, garden salads with herbed dressings, and fresh vegetables in season.

The Ardleys pride themselves on the special nature of the lodge; it is by no means "just another fishing camp," although it is famous for its Chinook salmon and that is its primary lure. River's Inlet is 35 miles long, rivaling Norway's fjords in beauty. The river's Chinook salmon are, for reasons unknown, genetically larger than Chinook from other river systems. In 1979 the average weight of a salmon taken here was 32 pounds. In addition to the fishing, the Ardleys offer scuba diving in the clear waters, scenic boat tours, clam digging, crab trapping, prawning, beachcombing, and digging for bottles at the ruins of old canneries. (This area was once a commercial fishing mecca, and in 1939 there were fourteen canneries at the inlet. All are gone now.) Jewel-like mountain lakes are within an easy hike, as are the maze of tiny islands and waters of the coves and bay. Sea otters, seals, and the occasional whale can be spotted here. The white sandy beaches are completely deserted; one can walk forever without meeting another person. This remote seaside vacation spot is well worth the extra effort and money it takes to get here.

Accommodations: 4 rooms with private bath. *Pets:* Not permitted. *Driving Instructions:* Daily scheduled seaplane flights from Vancouver Island (70 miles away) or charter flights from Vancouver Island (70 miles away) or charter flights from Vancouver (250 miles away). The "airport," known playfully as Sleepy Bay International, is a raft anchored just a few hundred yards from the lodge.

SURF LODGE

R.R. 1, Berry Point Road, Gabriola Island, British Columbia VOR 1XO, Canada. 604-247-9231. *Innkeepers:* David and Margaret Halliday. Open March through October (all year for groups).

Surf Lodge, a rustic resort at the edge of the blue water of the Strait of Georgia, is on the northern coast of Gabriola Island, twenty-five minutes from Nanaimo by ferry. Known for its sunset views, the lodge fronts on a rippled sandstone beach with many tidal pools and unusual rock formations; to its rear stretch 15 acres of unspoiled forest. The lodge was built in 1910 of large rocks and logs blending perfectly with the forest pines. Vines creep over porch railings fashioned of pooled branches. The interior is equally rustic in appearance. A large open lounge, the focal point of most indoor activities, is divided by a big fireplace whose rough stone chimney

reaches to the peeled-log ceiling. Comfortable antique furniture, overstuffed chairs, and picture windows add to the room's general appeal. The lounge, as in other northwest woods resorts, offers such rainy day amusements as table tennis, darts, an old piano, a radio, and a selection of books, cards, table games, and well-worn copies of *Beautiful British Columbia* magazine. This room and most of the guest rooms in the lodge overlook the Straits of Georgia and the ferries that ply busily between Vancouver and Nanaimo. All the rooms have been refurbished by the Hallidays and many now have queen-size beds. Nine rustic cabins dotting the seaward side of the lodge's secluded acreage are popular with families.

Before and after dinner, guests gravitate toward the Compass Room cocktail lounge, the best place to observe the outstanding summer sunsets. At the center of the room is a circular fireplace, which has a fire going most evenings. The Hallidays' home-cooked single-entree meals are served in a large, sunny dining room with picturesque ocean views. House specialties are Margaret's roast beef with Yorkshire pudding and the freshly caught salmon in season (summer and fall). Pies, breads, rolls, and soups are cooked up fresh in the kitchen. A special ritual here is teatime every afternoon at four.

Between the lodge and the sea is a large saltwater swimming pool. A number of resort-style lawn games are available, and for fishermen the Hallidays rent boats and motors and arrange for charter boats. The waters around the island teem with Coho salmon in late summer and all fall; ling cod is plentiful almost all year. The clear water and tortured rock formations make for excellent scuba diving. There are many quiet bays and forest paths, and the paved road around the island is ideal for joggers and bikers. The beaches and tidal pools offer up many treasures from the sea, even an occasional aboriginal artifact. Strangers to Gabriola and Surf Lodge always receive a warm welcome from the Hallidays and their staff.

Accommodations: 20 rooms, 9 in the lodge, the others in the 9 cabins; all have private bath. *Children:* Under four not permitted. *Pets:* Not permitted. *Driving Instructions:* The Gabriola Ferry leaves Nanaimo approximately every hour for a twenty-five-minute crossing. The lodge is 3 winding miles from the ferry slip. Guests can arrange to be met at the ferry.

Garibaldi

GARIBALDI LODGE

Garibaldi, British Columbia VON 3GO, Canada. 604-932-5222.
Innkeepers: John and Martha Lever. Open all year.

Garibaldi Lodge is on 8 acres bordering the Cheakamus River in southwestern British Columbia, adjacent to Garibaldi Village. Built in 1917, the lodge offers overnight accommodations in a rustic cedar-shingled lodge. Throughout the three-story building the walls are covered with the original cedar paneling, and there are comforters on every bed and other homelike touches. Most guest rooms are on the second and third floors; guests share a bath on each level. Family-style dining is the order here, with home-cooked, Quebec-style meals the specialties. Roast beef, boeuf bourguignon, and seafood casserole are among the Levers' favorites.

Garibaldi Lodge operates all year; many of its guests enjoy the fine downhill skiing at nearby Whistler Mountain, which has a vertical drop of more than 4,000 feet and some of the finest slopes in the province. There is excellent cross-country skiing in the Garibaldi Provincial Park; trails through the park leave from the lodge. Instruction is available at the Frank Ludtke Cross-Country Ski School.

In the warmer months the lodge provides a base for hiking in the Black Tusk Meadows–Garibaldi Lake area as well as for more serious mountaineering in the surrounding wilderness. There is still water and white water canoeing in the nearby lakes and Cheakamus River.

Accommodations: 14 rooms with hall bathrooms. Running water in rooms. *Pets:* Not permitted. *Driving Instructions:* The lodge is about 60 miles north of Vancouver, just off Route 99 in the village of Garibaldi.

CHILANKO LODGE

Route 20, Kleena Kleene, British Columbia V0L 1V0, Canada. Business office: 2511 116th Avenue N.E., Bellevue, WA 98004. Lodge phone: Ask operator for Kleena Kleen 2A. Business office phone: 206-822-9241. *Innkeeper:* Ragnar Gustafson. Open all year.

When we first heard of Chilanko Lodge, we wondered about the unusual name of its town. Our detective work turned up only that Kleena Kleen is derived from the local Indian word meaning "grease." Running through the town is the Klinaklini River, a spelling that is perhaps closer to the original word. Further heightening our interest in nomenclature, Chilanko Lodge stands at the edge of One Eye Lake. We were told with reasonable certainty that One Eye was a great Indian Chief who was drowned by the infamous Dalton gang in the lake that now bears his name. His grave stands at one end of it.

Chilanko Lodge is in a remote but accessible portion of British Columbia, not far from Tweedsmuir Provincial Park. The area is a popular spot with those seeking rustic summer vacations and with fishermen and hunters. As a result almost every town and many lodges have small grass landing strips. Chilanko Lodge may also be reached by car from Williams Lake, about 2½ hours to the east over a good gravel road that is maintained as part of the Trans-Canada Highway system. The main lodge was built in 1926, with additional cabins added over the ensuing years.

The lodge is a dormered log cabin with steps in front leading down to the lake. Guests arriving by plane may land at a 3,100-foot airstrip capable of handling DC-3s and all twin-engined planes. The lodge is rustic but warm and comfortable. A large fireplace surrounded by chairs dominates the living area. Meals at the lodge are served family-style from a menu that changes daily. Hors d'oeuvres precede the meal, which might feature a barbecue, standing rib roast, or turkey dinner, and which is accompanied by potatoes and vegetables, homemade breads and jams, salad, and dessert. Wine is available at the lodge.

Each guest room has either two twin or two double beds. In addition to the eight rooms in the main lodge, there are four cabins. The lodge is fully winterized and has indoor plumbing and a recently added sauna. Fishing probably leads the list of lodge activities, with salmon and steelback the most frequently caught species from the surrounding twelve lakes and streams. Hunting, boating, sailing, back-packing, hiking, horseback riding, cross-country skiing, ice fishing, sledding, and ice skating are also available at the lodge or nearby. The lodge provides opportunities nearby for wildlife photography, so it is recommended that guests bring cameras. As at many remote British Columbia lodges, rates are virtually all-inclusive. For example, summer rates include lodging, all meals, all local transportation to fishing lakes (except where float-plane trips are required), use of boats and motors on all local lakes, and the cleaning, preparing, or smoking of fish caught by guests.

Accommodations: 8 rooms and 4 cabins. *Pets:* Not permitted. *Driving Instructions:* Take Route 20 west from Williams Lake for about 150 miles to Kleena Kleene.

Ladysmith

YELLOW POINT LODGE

Yellow Point, Ladysmith, British Columbia. Mailing address: R. R. 3, Ladysmith, British Columbia VOR 2EO, Canada. 604-245-7422. *Innkeeper:* Gerry Hill. Open April 1 to October 31. Yellow Point Lodge is a testimony to the vision of one man, Gerry Hill. Returning from World War I and incarceration in a prisoner-of-war camp, Hill decided to settle in the Yellow Point region of coastal Vancouver Island. The 180-acre site was then and is now largely covered with virgin timber, from which Hill hewed his logs into the first and main building on the property. Completed in 1938 after two years of painstaking effort, the lodge is constructed of huge logs, many gables, and a main floor of wide-board fir that was installed on springs in the way the best dance floors were built half a century ago. The lodge's lounge has a large fieldstone fireplace and exposed-beam cathedral ceiling.

There are rooms in the main lodge and about thirty cottages scattered along the coastline nearby. Guest rooms are tucked here and there in the lodge; those in the gables have peaked ceilings. Many rooms are quite small; a few have private bathrooms. Hearty meals are served family-style in the lodge. Dinner is but one of six meals and

collations available at the lodge. In addition to breakfast and lunch, midmorning coffee and both afternoon and late-night tea are offered. Meals are included in the very reasonable American-plan rates. So are swims in the lodge's 235-foot, walled-off salt-water swimming pool just outside the front door. Other activities include tennis, volleyball, badminton, canoeing, rowboating, and sailing. One can walk or jog along trails through the lodge's acreage of virgin timber, past trees that are half a milennium old and more than 6 feet in diameter.

Accommodations: 41 rooms, 6 with private bath. *Pets and Children:* Not permitted. *Driving Instructions:* From Victoria, drive north on Route 1 through Ladysmith. Three miles north of town, take the turnoff to Yellow Point and go 6 miles to the lodge. From the north, take the Yellow Point turnoff 3 miles south of Nanaimo. The lodge is 12 miles to the south.

Likely

NORTHERN LIGHTS LODGE

Box 33, Likely, British Columbia VOL 1NO, Canada. 604-790-2200. *Innkeepers:* Frank and Julia Lolich. Open May 15 through October.

You know you are heading for adventure when you pass a place called 150 Mile House and still have 50 miles more to go on Cariboo Road. Your destination is Northern Lights Lodge, in central British Columbia on the shore of Lake Quesnel among birch, cedar, and fir trees. The log cabin lodge was built in 1945–47 and its site and adjoining properties were originally owned by a niece of Andrew Carnegie. Today the Northern Lights complex includes the lodge with its northern-woods look and guest accommodations, lounge–living room, and dining room; a few housekeeping units; and a small, secluded area set aside for house trailers. All overlook the lake.

The main lodge centers around its lounge–living room furnished with antiques of the area and groupings of overstuffed chairs and couches, many draped with animal skins. The couch in front of the imposing stone fireplace with its resident moose has a mountain-lion rug, head and all, thrown across its back. Pelts, horns, and trophy heads decorating the walls and beams—even the upright piano—are of beaver, fishers, lynx, coyote, bear, mink, marten, fox, muskrat, raccoon, birds of prey, and more. (These are local animals, and this is a fine spot for observing a wide variety of wildlife). The Lolichs offer complimentary cocktails before dinner in front of the hearth fire where guests gather to discuss the day's adventures. Meals are served family-style with one entree and plenty of food to assuage appetites sharpened by fresh northern air.

The simple and comfortable guest rooms in the lodge itself are entered from a private veranda and have private baths. The housekeeping cabins, outfitted with stoves and refrigerators, are furnished individually; some have antiques, animal rugs, antique guns, and local artifacts. A few of the rooms have Franklin stoves, and one has an old parlor stove.

The Northern Lights Lodge is remarkably well equipped for such a remote outpost. There are docking facilities for guests' boats and float planes, and boats and motors may be rented. The Lolichs maintain wilderness camps and cabins in an area accessible only by float planes. The lodge and country surrounding Lake Quesnel provide everything a big-game hunter, photographer, or fisherman could ask for. Also available are excellent trout fishing and white-water river rafting. There are guided historical and sightseeing tours of the unspoiled wilderness for which the Lolichs provide guides, cooks, and equipment.

Accommodations: 8 rooms, 4 with private bath. *Driving Instructions:* Turn east off Route 97 at 150 Mile House and follow the signs to Likely, about 50 miles along Cariboo Highway. The lodge is about 4 miles beyond Likely, on the shore of Lake Quensel. The journey is renowned for its scenic grandeur. There is an air-strip in Likely, just 3 miles from the camp. The lodge's float plane will pick guests up in Vancouver and land them on the lake in front of the lodge.

MAYNE ISLAND INN

Fernhill Road, Bennett Bay, Mayne Island, British Columbia VON 2JO, Canada. 604-539-2632 (Vancouver: 922-0138). *Innkeepers:* Anne and Weldon Pinchin. Open all year.

The southern portion of Vancouver Island is separated from the mainland by the Strait of Georgia, which contains a group of small islands long popular with local residents as vacation spots. One of these is Mayne Island, and the Mayne Island Inn is a good base for island vacationing. Built in 1912, the inn is not a fancy place but is run with panache by Weldon Pinchin, an innkeeper with a biography as romantic as any we know. A veteran sailor, he has not only run in eight Swiftsure races out of Victoria but has sailed the Atlantic in a 41-foot sailboat. Pinchin lived in the Yukon for twenty years and has panned for gold in the Klondike and worked on the Yukon River.

The inn, a white building with a touch of turn-of-the-century half-timbering, has a glass-enclosed sunporch—now known as the Wheelhouse—and a wooden sun deck popular with sunbathers, who also find the inn's 3 acres of waterfront property a convenient spot in which to soak up the welcome summer rays. Downstairs at the inn are a fireplace lounge with a color television set, a pub area, and a games room with a jukebox and pinball machines. The dining room, which seats about forty, is used for the evening meal. Every day several dishes are prepared for the choice of guests. Typical offerings are the special seafood platter, chicken or veal cordon bleu, pork chops, steaks, and on weekends, usually a roast of some sort. The dining room fireplace is up to even the chilliest days—it takes logs that are 6 feet long. Upstairs at the inn are twelve small and simply furnished guest rooms that share two common bathrooms. Seven of them have waterfront views and should be requested when reserving.

Guests at Mayne Island Inn are encouraged for bring fishing gear. One staff member is always happy to recommend the best fishing spots on the island. This is a fine place for cycling, so families might plan to bring along the family bicycles for more leisurely exploration.

Accommodations: 12 rooms with shared bath. *Pets:* Not permitted. *Driving Instructions:* Take either the Tsawwassen Ferry from the mainland or the Swartz Bay Ferry from Vancouver Island and disembark at Mayne Island terminal. Drive along Village Bay Road and turn right onto Fernhill Road, and proceed to Mayne Island Inn.

Qualicum Beach

THE GEORGE INN

P.O. Box 400, Qualicum Beach, British Columbia VOR 2TO, Canada. 604-752-9238. *Innkeepers:* Gerry and Sharon Bone and David and Eva Horsburgh. Open all year.

The George Inn, built in 1932 as the Sunset Inn, was one of the few older hotels remaining in Qualicum Beach after the old Qualicum Beach Hotel was torn down in 1972. In 1965 the Sunset was extensively remodeled and became the George, overlooking the Strait of Georgia and the Qualicum Beach golf course from its location on the eastern shore of Vancouver Island. Its decor is in Tudor style with a criss-cross of dark woods set in white stucco both inside and out, a look featured in much of the town. The building's main section has the look and feel of an old English inn. It has twenty-one small guest rooms, some with large canopied beds and baronial reproduction furnishings. In 1975 the innkeepers built a twenty-four room addition in the style of the older section; guest rooms here are modern in appearance with queen-size beds, television, and picture windows that open onto dark-wood balconies overlooking the grounds and sea.

The hotel dining room offers meals in a Tudor room warmed by fires in the large stone hearth. Old English banners and heraldry decorate the walls, and the furnishings, although reproductions, are much like those one would expect to find in a grand castle hall. House specialties are prime ribs and steak and kidney pie. A coffee shop in the hotel serves smaller meals and also has a fireplace.

The George has a Finnish sauna that guests can enjoy before jumping into the heated indoor swimming pool opening onto the patio. For those who prefer a more bracing swim, the beach is just three blocks from the hotel. The golf course is available to hotel guests, and tennis and fishing offer additional recreation. Boating is a favorite sport in this area; the Qualicum Boat House provides rentals. There is a curling rink next to the tennis courts for those interested in the more unusual sports.

Accommodations: 45 rooms with private bath. *Pets:* Only small, well-behaved pets permitted. *Driving Instructions:* The hotel is 30 miles north of Nanaimo. There is bus service from Victoria and Nanaimo on the Island Coach Lines. The Canadian Pacific Ferry from Vancouver carries private cars to Nanaimo.

QUALICUM COLLEGE INN

College Road, Qualicum Beach, Vancouver Island, British Columbia. Mailing address: P.O. Box 99, Qualicum Beach, British Columbia VOR 2TO, Canada. 604-752-9262. *Innkeeper:* Kerry Keilty. Open all year.

Arriving at Qualicum College Inn is rather like pulling up at an English country hotel. Ivy surrounds the heavy oak doors of the three-story, red-roofed timber and stucco building. This Vancouver Island hostelry had interesting beginnings. Qualicum College was a boys' private boarding school from 1935 until 1970. The school's founder and headmaster for its full tenure, Mr. Ivan Knight, lives near the inn and can often be seen strolling its grounds. His school was grounded in what he called the "seven C's" of education: Christianity, classics, cricket, cadet corps, cold baths, courtesy, and corporal punishment. At a recent reunion of the Old Boys who had graduated in the past thirty-five years, tales of the good old days were told reflecting the warmth and affection his students feel for Mr. Knight. In 1970 the school was forced to close; it was converted two years later into an inn.

Extensive renovations were made to create more spacious quarters for guests than had been provided for the boys, while maintaining the medieval feeling of the inn's interior. The photographs decorating the dining room are from the school archives, and the Prefect's Lounge contains many trophies and pieces of school equipment. There are modern touches like wall-to-wall carpeting in guest rooms, and private baths as well as comfortable beds of recent vintage. The medieval theme of the dining room, accentuated by heavy dark-wood chairs and heraldic items on the walls, is carried through in the specialty of the house: a medieval meal with a number of traditional "removes" or selections. It starts with a country peasant soup, is followed by a platter of fresh seafood that might contain crab, oysters, and salmon, and proceeds to hearth-roasted chicken Henry VIII–style. It concludes with assorted fruit and a cheese board. For those whose preferences lean to more recent centuries, a large à la carte menu lists starters including shrimp Mary Rose (with avocado and a special sauce), coquilles Saint Jacques, pâté with aspic, and Russian caviar. The numerous entrees include roast beef, several steaks, king crab, curried shrimp, trout, salmon, and beef Wellington. Of the several desserts, there is one we can never resist— English trifle.

Qualicum College Inn was the location for a 1977 made-for-television movie entitled *It Happened at Lakewood Manor* and starring Myrna Loy. On a more regular basis, the inn features jazz weekends that have attracted such artists as George Shearing, Cannon Ball Adderley, Ramsey Lewis, and Louis Bellson. At Qualicum College you are transported back into another time, or rather to a number of earlier times. Its proximity to the ocean and its pleasant grounds are bonuses, as are their whirlpool bath, Finnish sauna, and heated swimming pool.

A number of special packages are offered by the inn. Newlyweds might consider the Homeymoon package which includes three nights, breakfast in bed, champagne on arrival, a ride on a tandem bicycle, and more.

Accommodations: 50 rooms, 48 with private bath. *Driving Instructions:* Take Route 19 about 30 miles north of Nanaimo.

Quilchena

QUILCHENA HOTEL

Quilchena, British Columbia VOE 2RO, Canada. 604-378-2611.
Innkeepers: Mr. and Mrs. Guy Rose. Open first weekend in May to first weekend in October.

At the turn of the century, Joseph Guichon was already a wealthy man. Having made a fortune from his cattle empire, he had another plan. Word was out that a spur connecting the Canadian Pacific main line to Princeton was to be constructed and would pass through his Quilchena Ranch. In 1908, Guichon set out to build a fine hotel, to be ready for its first guests by the time the spur was completed. But the route terminated at Nicola, and for a time it appeared that the hotel would stand empty. Joseph Guichon was undaunted; he opened his doors to the horse-and-carriage trade. Soon known as the "in" spot of its day, the Quilchena Hotel's rooms and saloon were filled until 1919, when Prohibition put an end to its thriving trade. At that time Guichon and his family moved into the building; it remained a private dwelling until 1958, when the third generation of the family began to restore it. It reopened for business in 1962 and is today a popular summer "get-away" hotel.

Surrounded by one of the largest working cattle ranches in the province and overlooking Nicola Lake, the hotel has been restored in a way that maintains its historic feeling. Each room has been decorated individually with old family antiques, ornamental iron bedsteads, and the original lighting fixtures. The saloon retains its original hardwood bar complete with brass foot-rail, spittoons, and bullet holes in the woodwork. The dining room serves a different ranch-style meal every day. Typical offerings include roast beef, roast turkey, ham, cabbage rolls, and T-bone steaks.

Several recreational activities are available to guests. Nicola Lake offers swimming, boating, and fishing. There is a nine-hole golf course just out the back door that charges greens fees, and horses are available for rent.

Accommodations: 14 rooms share two baths. *Pets:* Not permitted. *Driving Instructions:* Take the Trans-Canada Highway (Route 1) to Kamloops; then drive south on Route 5 about 45 miles to Quilchena.

Riske Creek

CHILCOTIN LODGE

Riske Creek, British Columbia VOL 1TO, Canada. *Telephone:* Ask operator for Riske Creek 2N. *Innkeeper:* Sandara Bardua. Open all year.

Chilcotin Lodge is a log building off the highway about a quarter mile up a hill overlooking a valley. It is in the center of the Chilcotin ranch-lands and offers country-style guest accommodations. They were in the middle of renovations when we inquired, so the description for this edition must, of necessity, be brief. The lodge offers a friendly, homelike atmosphere with a large guest parlor that has a stone fire-place. Family-style meals are served in the dining room, but a new menu will be announced when renovations are completed in May 1980. Guests traveling to this part of the province are urged to call first to see how the renovation work has progressed.

Accommodations: 10 rooms with shared bath. *Driving Instructions:* The lodge is 30 miles west of Williams Lake, British Columbia, on Route 20.

Rossland

THE RAM'S HEAD INN

Red Mountain Ski Area, Rossland, British Columbia. Mailing address: Box 636, Rossland, British Columbia VOG 1YO, Canada. 604-362-9577. *Innkeepers:* Doreen and Dave Butler. Open all year.

Red Mountain Ski Area, encompassing Paradise Basin, Granite Mountain, and Red Mountain, is to the north of the northeastern border of the state of Washington. The Ram's Head Inn, the mountain's newest lodge, is a cedar-paneled modern building with clean lines and natural pine color surrounded by pines and mossy banks in the quiet of its own 4½ acres. Lifts for downhill skiing are just 200 meters away. Snow lends a special magic to the property. Inside the lodge, guests are drawn to the cedar-paneled lounge where fires burn all year. Sunlight filters through the pines and the room's big picture windows. Skier-size home-cooked meals served in the inviting lounge beside the fire consist of one entree with generous side dishes; guests serve themselves family-style. Bedrooms off the lounge look out into the pines and are furnished with queen-size or twin beds. A sauna is provided for relaxation.

The Butlers, devoted ski enthusiasts, have installed a well-equipped cross-country ski shop in the lodge with rentals and ski workshops. Trails begin at the doorstep and at the nearby parking lot. For a more daring and exciting ski experience, the Butlers direct guests to the Valkyrie Heli-ski. Helicopters drop experienced skiers and highly qualified guides in remote wilderness mountain terrains. Many of these adventurous skiers make the Ram's Head their home base, so interested guests are bound to hear all about such exotic-sounding places as the Valkyrie, Battle Range with its granite spires in the heart of the Selkirks, and the Monashees. Red Mountain Ski Area has a wide variety of conditions for downhill skiers of all levels of experience—from the long, easy slopes of Squaw Basin to the highspeed international downhill skiing on Buffalo Ridge and Mountain Chief. In warm weather the area is a hikers' and nature lovers' delight. Endless marked and unmarked trails afford quick glimpses of the abundant and varied wildlife.

Rossland was called "Golden City" because of the area's rich veins of gold. The town, the gateway to the Kootenays, features a number of historic tours and sights. The Rossland Historical Museum displays mining and historical artifacts; a section of the old LeRoi Mine is open for underground tours.

Accommodations: 8 rooms with private bath. *Pets:* Not permitted. *Children:* Permitted, but the inn is more suited to adults. *Driving Instructions:* From Rossland, go west on Route 3B about 3 miles to the Red Mountain Ski Area turnoff. The inn is at the base of the hill.

LORD JIM'S LODGE

Ole's Cove Road, Sechelt, British Columbia. Mailing address: R.R. 1, Halfmoon Bay, British Columbia, Canada. 604-885-2232 (toll-free in Vancouver: 604-687-8212). *Innkeepers:* Hans and Chris Kuck and Hugh and Catherine Gadsby. Open all year.

Recently constructed, rustic Lord Jim's Lodge offers contemporary guest rooms and individual cottages in a scenic setting. The lodge has a peeled-log dining room with picture windows overlooking the rugged coastline. Twelve guest rooms with private baths are in the lodge, and the remainder are in individual cabins that have from one to three bedrooms each. The lodge's dining room offers a selection of local and imported seafood including Pacific salmon, smoked salmon, scallops, and shrimp. There are saunas, a heated swimming pool, and a games room. Many guests are drawn to the inn for its proximity to excellent fishing in most months of the year. The lodge offers guided salmon-fishing charters in Pender Harbor. Fish taken from the waters near the lodge include bluebacks, spring, and Coho salmon.

Accommodations: 31 rooms, 21 with private bath. *Pets:* Not permitted. *Driving Instructions:* Take the Trans-Canada Highway (Route 1) to Horseshoe Bay, just north of Vancouver, then board the Langdale Ferry to Langdale Landing. Proceed on Route 101 north to Lord Jim's Lodge, 14 miles north of Sechelt village.

Shawnigan Lake

SHAWNIGAN LAKE COUNTRY CLUB

Shawnigan Lake, British Columbia. Mailing address: P.O. Box 40, Shawnigan Lake, British Columbia VOR 2WO, Canada. 604-743-2312. Open mid-June to mid-September; open winter weekends and special holidays.

Shawnigan Lake Country Club, a large English-style country retreat, has large public rooms with high ceilings and windows that overlook the lake. The foyer, carpeted in red, has wood paneling, bookshelves filled with books, and a stone fireplace surrounded by comfortable sofas. Adjoining is a large dining room and lounge that was recently renovated by the management. The dining room, almost completely surrounded by windows overlooking the lake, opens onto a sun deck where many guests take their meals in the warmer months. The main building contains only three guest rooms; remaining overnight rooms are in the adjoining Robin Hood annex. Most rooms at the resort are fairly small and simple, with comfortable furnishings and an old-fashioned look. The grounds surrounding the buildings are attractively landscaped and well maintained; lawns lead to freshly painted fences, weeping willow trees, and, in the background, the pines and firs indigenous to the region.

Guests on the American plan are offered a single entree of the day at dinnertime, but there is also an à la carte menu featuring an assortment of steaks, seafood, poultry, and chops.

The main attraction of this country-resort inn is the great variety of activities available. Because of its location on the lake and its 500 feet of sandy beach, many summer guests stay at the inn for the water sports alone. There are sailing, rowboating, paddle boating, and canoeing as well as waterskiing and sailboat instruction. The inn offers badminton, outdoor shuffleboard, two tennis courts, and a par-three nine-hole golf course. The room charge includes use of all facilities and necessary equipment, except for an additional fee for water skiing. A special summer program for children includes picnic trips to Memory Island and many group sports. Grownups are free to enjoy the resort knowing that their children are under expert care all day. Another enjoyable excursion is to Whippletree Junction, between Shawnigan Lake and Duncan. Old-time ice cream parlors, a tattoo shop, and crafts are available there, and an auction is held every Sunday in the summer.

Accommodations: 30 guest rooms, 12 with private bath. *Pets:* Not permitted. *Driving Instructions:* From Vancouver, take the ferry to Sidney. Drive south on Route 17 to Victoria, and then take Route 1 (Trans-Canada Highway) to Mill Bay. Turn left onto the Shawnigan–Mill Bay Road and drive to the village of Shawnigan. Turn right on the Renfrew Road and drive to the inn.

Stubbs Island

CLAYOQUOT LODGE

Stubbs Island, British Columbia. Mailing address: P.O. Box 188, Tofino, British Columbia V0N 1B0, Canada. 604-725-3284. *Inn-keeper:* Lucas Stiefvater. Open mid-May to mid-September.

Clayoquot Sound off Vancouver Island was first charted by Captain Cook in the late 1700s on the same voyage that saw the discovery of British Columbia. In the ensuing years, the Sound became an import-

ant shipping lane for the British merchant navy, which was engaged in a lucrative but hazardous fur trade with the coastal Indians. This trade first brought Captain Pinney of the merchant navy to the area, where, surrounded by waters littered with shipwrecks, he set up a ship chandlery in 1875, on an island he had traded from the Indians for a barrel of molasses. Thirty years later the Clayoquot Lodge was built, a white, English shingle building at the edge of the sea and reached only by sea. Most guests drive or fly to Tofino and then are picked up by the lodge's motor launch, the M.V. Duke. Others arrive by seaplane at the lodge's own dock.

Clayoquot Lodge maintains its rustic, turn-of-the-century atmosphere with exposed beam ceilings, cedar paneling, a fieldstone fireplace, wicker and bent-bamboo furniture, and caned ceiling lamps. Guest rooms have print wallpapers and, like the lodge as a whole, a mixture of antiques and contemporary furniture. The dining room, highly respected for the quality of its food, has checkered tablecloths and a variety of local dishes emphasizing fresh seafood, such as Tofino crab, salmon, cod, red snapper, and local oysters. The public is welcome to dine at the lodge at the evening meals.

Stubbs Island's 140 acres include a 20-acre sand pit whose dunes slope down, on one side, to some very fine clam-digging flats. The island is a miniature rain forest with several trails leading from the rocky shores to sandy beaches and finally to the evergreen forest of the interior. Around the lodge, the grounds have large rhododendron bushes and lawns bordered by a variety of flowers. Although the island's natural beauty affords ample relaxation and entertainment, there are also more organized activities. Charter fishing trips operate out of Tofino, and McCully Aviation offers scenic flights. Guests may go to Hot Springs Cove for a natural hot bath in the wilderness; museum buffs should enjoy Tofino's Marine Museum.

Accommodations: 8 rooms with private bath. *Pets:* Not permitted. *Driving Instructions:* Take Route 4 from Port Alberni to Tofino. Upon arrival at Tofino, call the lodge for pickup by its launch.

Victoria

THE CAPTAIN'S PALACE

309 Belleville Street, Victoria, British Columbia V8V 1X2, Canada. 604-388-9191. *Innkeeper:* Mrs. Florence Prior. Open all year.

The Captain's Palace bills itself as Victoria's smallest hotel; with only one suite available for overnight accommodations, it certainly qualifies. But despite its size, it is worthy of mention. The Captain's Palace was built in 1897 as a sumptuous home for one of Victoria's first and leading industrialists. W. J. Pendray. At the time it was considered one of the finest structures in the new province's capital. Only a few changes have been made to the original building, and every detail of the home has been restored and carefully preserved by its present owner, Florence Prior. Overlooking Victoria's Inner Harbor, the Captain's Palace is filled with crystal chandeliers, stained-glass windows, hand-frescoed high ceilings, and other memories of an earlier era. Its details set this place apart: the richly paneled rooms, elaborate mantled fireplace, and the collection of antiques displayed in a built-in buffet and throughout seven intimate dining rooms.

Each dining room is special. The Library has a hidden panel door. Upstairs, the Harbor Room has fine views of the water. The menu includes oysters Rockefeller, Neptune sole (rolled around tiny local shrimp and poached in white wine), and fresh salmon steaks, as well as veal cordon bleu, Cornish game hen, chicken, and a steak and lobster combination. One favorite house dessert is their Venetian cream, a marriage of ice cream, brandy, and liqueurs. The inn's serving personnel are dressed in frilled "Upstairs-Downstairs" apparel.

A well-kept secret at the Captain's Palace is its two-room luxury suite on the second floor. The suite offers a night in a hand-carved, two-hundred year old oak bed, private dining under hand-frescoed ceilings, and an old-fashioned bell-pull that summons a pinafored maid. The room rate includes a full "eggs 'n bacon" breakfast and complimentary gifts.

Accommodations: A 2-room suite with private bath. *Pets:* Not permitted. *Children:* Permitted, but no facilities for very young children. *Driving Instructions:* The inn is in downtown Victoria, three blocks west of the legislative buildings.

THE EMPRESS HOTEL

721 Government Street, Victoria, British Columbia V8W 1W5, Canada. 604-384-8111. *Innkeeper:* Canadian Pacific Hotels. Open all year.

When the Empress Hotel opened in Victoria in 1908 it took immediate claim to the title "Queen of the Province." Nothing has changed in the past seventy years to dethrone the Empress, and a stay here is to step back into an earlier era of elegance and service. This is, like all Canadian Pacific hotels, a full-size, in-town hotel. Set back amid well-kept gardens at the harbor's edge, the Empress is the first thing guests from Seattle and Port Angeles see when they arrive at the docks. The hotel is an imposing sight; ivy covers the arched entrance to its main lobby, a favorite meeting place for the fashionable, who wait on fine Victorian furniture surrounded by white columns. The Empress's guest rooms are fitting for the traveler demanding a first-class experience in hotel accommodations. Rooms are spacious; many have separate sitting rooms with fine furnishings, wall-paneling, and twentieth-century comforts like color television and air conditioning.

Just exploring the Empress is fun. Off the lobby are two bars: the Library with its book-lined walls and leather; and the Bengal Lounge, where a tigerskin hangs on the wall above the fireplace. One can eat at the famed Empress Dining Room or the less expensive Garden Café in the lower lobby.

Perhaps once you have decided to come to the Empress, it makes sense to continue to go first class and eat under the carved ceiling of the Empress Room. Specialties include salmon served poached, broiled with spinach, or as Coulibiac—the Russian presentation of salmon in an envelope of brioche. Roast beef is served with Yorkshire pudding and horseradish sauce. Another popular offering is crab and shrimp Empress, blending the seafood with brandy and mornay sauce. The Empress offers a lavish buffet dinner every Thursday and Sunday except July and August. Included are most salads one could name, an array of cold cuts, two hot dishes as well as a baron of beef (or during Christmas a roast turkey and ham), plus a selection of vegetables. Desserts are chosen from a separate dessert table laden with sweets.

If discotheque is your cup of tea, Tiffany's on the lower level is popular with the younger dancing crowd. Afternoon tea at the Empress is a long-established tradition. It is served in the main lobby, and the daily ceremony is crowded with tourists during the summer months. If you are planning a trip to Vancouver Island at Christmas,

you might want to investigate the hotel's four-day, eighteenth-century-style Christmas package, which begins December 23 and continues with holiday festivities until December 27.

Accommodations: 416 rooms and suites, most with private bath.

OAK BAY BEACH HOTEL

1175 Beach Drive, Victoria, British Columbia V8S 2N2, Canada. 604-598-4556. *Innkeeper:* Bruce R. Walker. Open all year.

Oak Bay Beach Hotel, overlooking the Oak Bay region of Victoria, is the city's only seaside hotel. On the oceanside, the grounds run from the gardens near the building to the shoreline, with views of the islands in the distance. Oak Bay Beach Hotel, originally built in 1928 as a hostelry for the elite of the province, burned to the ground two years later. It was rebuilt immediately and remains virtually untouched today. The shingle-roofed building is traditionally half-timbered and has numerous gables and smaller dormers jutting out along its roofline.

Inside the hotel are polished ceiling beams, fine woodwork and rugs, and other appointments befitting its stature. Many guest rooms have antique furnishings and are named after members of English royalty. The King Henry VIII suite has a four-poster, canopied brass bed—the only brass canopy-bed we have seen. The Georgian Suite blends period antiques and half-timbering with a modern sliding door that opens onto a small balcony with a view. The room named for Queen Elizabeth I has a pair of brass beds separated by an early table lamp. The hotel notes that the antiques selected for each room were mostly collected in England and generally reflect the period indicated by the room's name.

As expected of any English seaside hotel, fires burn in fireplaces in the lobby, lounge, and the Tudor dining room. A Continental menu offers many items named, like the rooms, for periods of history: Samuel Pepys brochette, for example, is a seafood entree served on a bed of rice. Naturally, the house specialty is roast prime ribs of beef with Yorkshire pudding. Among other beef entrees are chateaubriand, filet mignon, and beef Wellington. They serve a rack of locally raised lamb and a cross section of seafood including local salmon (in season) and Alaskan king crab. Anglophiles are drawn to the Snug, an English-style cocktail lounge that offers drink and such English fare as fish and chips, beefsteak and kidney pie, steak and other sandwiches, as well as daily pub specials.

Guests do not have far to go for formalized recreation. There is fine golfing at the nearby Victoria Oak Bay Golf Club, fishing in the Oak Bay Marina, and both swimming and tennis at the Oak Bay Recreation Centre, and just moments away lies the entire city of Victoria.

Accommodations: 50 rooms with private bath. *Pets:* Not permitted. *Driving Instructions:* In Victoria, take Dallas Road or Oak Bay Avenue to Beach Drive and the hotel.

OLDE ENGLAND INN

429 Lampson Street, Victoria, British Columbia V9A 5Y9, Canada. 604-388-4353. *Innkeepers:* Cyril and Darlene Lane. Open all year.

In 1946, Sam and Rosina Lane journeyed from Yorkshire, England, to Canada in search of a mansion that they could transform into a formal English guesthouse. Their search ended at the estate of another Yorkshireman, T. M. Slater. In 1909, Slater had commissioned Samuel McLure, one of Victoria's finest architects, to design a Tudor-style mansion. English and Scottish craftsmen were brought to Canada specially to construct the home in the Old World tradition. The Lanes immediately set about restoring and converting the residence into an inn that could also serve as a repository of their impressive collection of English and European antiques and decorative arts.

The impression of entering a museum is brought into focus when one steps into the inn's Baronial Hall. Suits of armor, ancient swords, and carved dining chairs and tables are displayed in a setting of hand-rubbed paneling and exposed beams. The dining table is set before a fireplace whose gleaming copper canopy is flanked by bricks.

The baronial feeling extends to the guest rooms, of which the "King's Rooms" represent the ultimate in lavish settings. The Royal Albert Room, for example, is furnished with a 12-foot oak half-tester bed that was once used by Queen Victoria and her beloved consort. A floor-to-ceiling stone fireplace stands next to the mid-nineteenth-century fluted-brass canopied four-poster bed in the Prince Charles Room. Although Elizabeth I may not have slept in the imposing carved-oak canopy bed in the room bearing her name, the appointments surely befit a queen. French antiques from the Louis XIV period set the tone of the King Edward VII room, which is dominated by a gilt-topped canopy bed draped in purple velvet. The bed was used by the monarch in Warwick Castle.

Dining at the Olde England Inn is in keeping with the building's mood and decor. Heading the menu is roast baron of beef with Yorkshire pudding, followed by an English mixed grill, traditional English steak and kidney or chicken pies, as well as such North American offerings as trout, liver and bacon, T-bone steak, or a lobster and steak combination. One may begin the meal with such offerings as clear green turtle soup or Scotch vegetable soup, escargots, shrimps, or oysters and end with sherry trifle, apple pie, black-currant tarts, and other sweets. English-style eating does not

commence at nightfall: there are full English breakfasts (including kippers) and a full selection of hot and cold English traditional and pub-style lunches, not to mention full English afternoon teas.

From the very beginning the Lanes' plan was to "create a real English Village of the Elizabethan period." As a result, the inn is now part of a major tourist attraction that comprises a number of replicas of important buildings from throughout England. Typical of the Lanes' attention to their project is the minutely detailed replica of Anne Hathaway's thatch roof home with its English gardens. The Lanes even grew their own wheat for the roof, then imported a skilled English thatcher to complete the task. Down Chaucer Lane, guests will find the Harvard House, home of the mother of John Harvard, who endowed the university. Next door is the Garrick Inn, a full-size replica of the inn immortalized by John David Garrick of theatrical fame. The Olde Curiosity Shop, a replica of the 1594 shop celebrated by Charles Dickens, now offers old and new gifts for sale. An English "bobby" directs traffic, which often becomes congested in this popular tourist spot. We suspect you will agree that this inn is like no other in North America.

Accommodations: 48 rooms with private bath. *Driving Instructions:* Cross the Johnson Street Bridge onto Esquimalt Road heading west. Turn left on Lampson Street at the fifth stop light. The inn is four blocks down the street on the left.

WILDERNESS LODGE

P.O. Box 4758, Williams Lake, British Columbia V2G 2V8, Canada. Radiotelephone number 98880, JK channel via Williams Lake radio operator. *Innkeeper:* Manfred Zilliken. Open May 1 to September 30.

Getting to Wilderness Lodge conjures up memories of the old joke ending "You can't get there from here." In truth, like all remote Canadian lodges, Wilderness can be reached by air from a reasonably accessible village—in this case Williams Lake. The lodge is at the end of the east arm of Quesnel Lake, about 80 miles east of Williams Lake. As with remote lodges in the Northwest Territories and elsewhere in Canada, a stay here is relatively expensive; however, prices include all meals and available activities.

Wilderness Lodge consists of a main lodge and four cabins, each an A-frame-style building constructed of cedar and other native logs. The feeling is decidedly rustic with custom handmade cedar furniture, fireplaces in the dining room, living room, and bar, but there are such modern comforts as carpeting throughout. Each cabin has a working fireplace and hot-water shower. Dining at Wilderness Lodge is family-style, with roasts, chicken and turkey, and homemade stews heading the list of offerings.

Activities at Wilderness are in keeping with its remote location at the end of a 68-mile-long lake. There is excellent fishing throughout the summer season with rainbow trout, lake trout (char), and Dolly Varden leading the list. All boats, motors, and gas are provided as part of the basic lodge rates. Sailing, water skiing, canoeing, and horseback riding are also available. The lakefront lodge is surrounded by the Canadian Rockies, which rise from 600 to 9,00 feet, and three-day trail rides deep into the mountains are available to lodge guests. Guests may also go mountain climbing, hunt, go trapshooting, or take nature walks to see the abundant fauna and flora.

Accommodations: 9 lodge rooms, plus 4 cabins. Rooms in the lodge have shared bath. *Driving Instructions:* You cannot get to the lodge directly by car. Guests usually drive to Williams Lake and get a charter flight to the lodge, which has its own airstrip; planes can land on the field and float planes can land on the lake. There is boat pickup at Lowny's Lodge or Elysia Resort on Quesnel Lake.

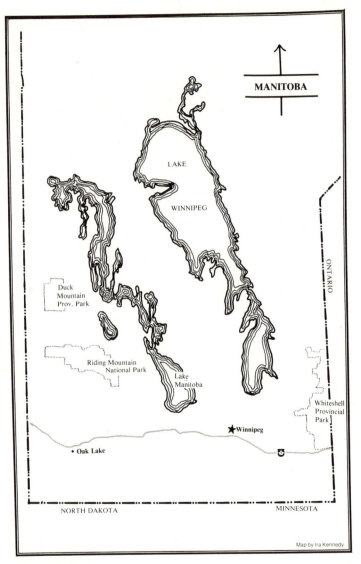

MANITOBA

LAKE

WINNIPEG

Duck
Mountain
Prov. Park

Riding Mountain
National Park

Lake
Manitoba

ONTARIO

Whiteshell
Provincial
Park

★Winnipeg

• Oak Lake

NORTH DAKOTA

MINNESOTA

Map by Ira Kennedy

Manitoba

MAXANNE ROLLING ACRES FARM

R.R. 1, Oak Lake, Manitoba ROM 1PO, Canada. 204-855-2713.
Innkeepers: Max and Annie Gompf. Open May to October 1.

When Max and Annie Gompf bought their 1906 fieldstone farmhouse in the 1940s, it was in need of total modernization. They added running water and electricity, papered and painted the walls and woodwork, carpeted the downstairs, reupholstered the furniture, and readied the place for their first guests. They turned one room downstairs into a den. It has wooden beams made by Max and a display case filled with the many Indian artifacts that the Gompfs and their guests have found on the farm, not far from the buildings. In the days before the white man settled Manitoba, this was a popular buffalo-hunting spot for midwestern tribes, who would migrate to the area each summer.

Rolling Acres is very much the Gompf's home, and they treat you like family guests while you are here. They have taken pictures of almost everyone who has stayed at the farm, and albums full of photos await the browser. Over the years Max and Annie have been proud to welcome guests of every race and religion from all corners of North America and Europe.

Meals at Rolling Acres are served on request. Phone ahead and Annie will have dinner (the noon meal) or supper waiting when you arrive. Meals run to typical hearty meat-potatoes-and-fresh-vegetable farm food. Annie bakes all her own bread and makes jams and jellies as well as cookies and cakes. Most meals are served in the large kitchen except, as Annie says, "When Europeans come they are served in the dining room, as is their fashion."

Max and Annie have a happy farm (they no longer farm the land themselves but rent it to a neighbor farmer). The children of guests enjoy pony rides bareback style and are taken fishing at Assinaborne River 2 miles away. The Gompfs and their guests will frequently spend an afternoon at Oak Lake Beach, 18 miles to the south.

Accommodations: 5 rooms with shared baths. *Driving Instructions:* Take the Trans-Canada Highway (Route 1) west from Brandon to the junction of Route 21. Turn north on Route 21 and go north and east for 9.6 miles through the Sioux Valley Indian Reserve; then turn south on a gravel road and go 5½ miles to the farm gate. Guests often call ahead at the Gulf station at the junction of Routes 1 and 21.

Winnipeg

MARLBOROUGH INN

331 Smith Street, Winnipeg, Manitoba R3B 2G9, Canada. 204-942-6411. *Innkeeper:* Delta Hotels Ltd. Open all year.

The Marlborough Inn, a moderately large member of the Delta Hotel chain, was originally opened in 1914 as the Olympica Hotel, combining fine marble from Italy, polished stone from France, and stained-glass windows and doors from England. Closed during World War I, it reopened soon thereafter and was renamed the Marlborough in 1920. It remains a "grand old lady," an impressive reminder of an earlier Winnipeg era.

Characteristic of the traditional ambience at the Marlborough is Churchills, the hotel's formal dining room, which has a two-story-high vaulted ceiling, warm wood paneling, and two-tiered candelabra-style brass chandeliers. Boldly colored upholstered chairs surround small dining tables illuminated by the chandeliers and by daylight coming through tall stained-glass windows. Portraits of the Churchills hang in tribute to that distinguished family. All this combines to produce a clublike setting for the enjoyment of the inn's specialties, including steak au poivre, escalope de veau Philadelphia, entrecôte Kodiak, and whole Dover sole amandine. In all there are almost twenty entrees. In addition to several soups, appetizers include prawns armagnac, smoked salmon crepes, escargots, British Columbia smoked salmon, and lobster cocktail.

The more informal Flanders Cafe also has stained glass and a row of wrought-iron lamps. The original bar here, called the "longest bar in North America," was the birthplace of the Canadian Legion. Guests may enjoy drinks in the Colonel Webb Lounge in a setting that includes a heavy beamed ceiling, brick and tile walls and pillars, and a marble stairway.

The guest rooms have been fully renovated in recent years and combine campaign-style furniture with modern beds covered with bold prints. The rooms have air conditioning, color television, and modern baths with king-size towels and fist-size bars of soap. The hotel's several suites include a parlor and one or two adjoining bedrooms.

Accommodations: 144 rooms with private bath. *Driving Instructions:* Take the Trans-Canada Highway to Portage Avenue (the main thoroughfare through Winnipeg); then drive on Portage to Smith Street. The hotel is half a block off Portage.

New Brunswick

Evandale

EVELEIGH HOTEL

Route 102, Evandale, New Brunswick. Mailing address: R.R. 1, Hampstead, New Brunswick EOG 1YO, Canada. 506-425-9993 or 506-425-2591. *Innkeepers:* Frank and Gloria Arris. Open all year. In 1890 road travelers were brought across the river at Evandale by the cable ferry operated by John O. VanWart, the proprietor of a pub just down the river. His success as ferryboat captain and with his pub led him to build the Evandale Hotel in that year. Hotel and ferry have both survived almost a century and can be enjoyed by present-day guests as much as by their predecessors.

Renamed the Eveleigh Hotel in the 1940s, the white-shingled Victorian structure has its red roof broken by three bay-windowed dormers that face the river. Eveleigh likes to call itself the "last of the riverboat hotels," and it certainly harkens back to days gone by. On its dining room walls are numerous old pictures of the hotel dating from the turn of the century. In the riverboat days, the dining room was a frequent lunch stop for boats between the Bay of Fundy and Grand Lake to the interior. More recently a number of rustic cabins

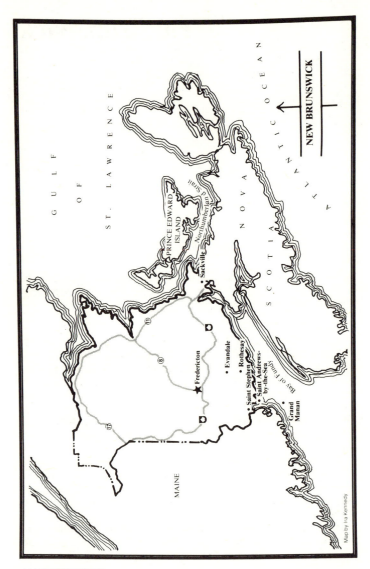

NEW BRUNSWICK

GULF OF ST. LAWRENCE

ATLANTIC OCEAN

PRINCE EDWARD ISLAND

Northumberland Strait

NOVA SCOTIA

Sackville

Fredericton ★

Evandale

Rothesay

Saint Stephen

Saint Andrews-by-the-Sea

Grand Manan

Bay of Fundy

MAINE

Map by Ira Kennedy

and more modern motel units have been added, but guest rooms in the main hotel are still available for overnight guests. These are furnished mostly with antiques, and many of the beds have handmade quilts.

Guests tend to return to the Eveleigh for its old-fashioned New Brunswick home-style cooking. It is all done by Mrs. Arris, except for the pastries, pies, and rolls, for which she employs a respected local cook. Vegetables at the inn are grown locally and served in season. Food is simple and filling, with scallops, seafood casserole, roast turkey, and English-style steak and mushrooms heading the list. There is also a sandwich menu as well as homemade soups and a number of desserts.

Accommodations: 15 rooms in the hotel, 5 with private bath. Additional rooms in motels and cabins. *Pets:* Permitted in cabins and motels only. *Driving Instructions:* Take Route 102 to Evandale. The hotel is at the Evandale ferry (Route 124) on Route 102.

Grand Manan Island

Grand Manan calls itself the Queen of the Fundy Isles, and with good reason. Acres of wildflower meadows run to the edge of cliffs dropping precipitously to the surf below; tiny fishing villages dot the coastline; birds abound—James Audubon logged 300 species during a visit in 1833. In just a few minutes you can gather enough wild berries to satisfy even the most greedy. Grand Manan is practically unspoiled. You can drive all day and never see a neon sign. What you do see are happy, friendly people, most of whom make their living from the sea. Each day, fishing boats pull into docks along the coast to unload lobster, scallops, halibut, bluefish, cod, and herring. Even seaweed is harvested for use in foods and medicine by these islanders, who recognize the boundless riches of the Atlantic. Grand Manan is a place for naturalists, photographers, and artists. Hiking and beach-combing are by far more likely activities than the nightlife of mainland cities. Those who come in the summer might like to investigate the nature school offered by the Grand Manan Museum, which also features the Moses Collection of Grand Manan birds and exhibits displays of local history and geology. Grand Harbour has several little island-crafts shops.

GRAND HARBOUR INN

Grand Harbour, Grand Manan, New Brunswick EOG 1XO, Canada. Off-season mailing address: P.O. Box 110, MacDonald College, Province of Quebec, H9X 1CO, Canada. 506-662-8681 (off-season: 514-457-9190). *Innkeeper:* Mrs. M. E. Murphy. Open June, July, and August.

The Grand Harbour Inn is a white Victorian island house set behind a traditional white-picket fence. Its eaves and overhangs carry neat rows of gingerbread trim, and the third floor has large dormers and a scallop treatment to the façade. One guest room overlooks a tiny second-floor veranda also trimmed with gingerbread. The innkeeper-owner, Mrs. Murphy, prides herself on treating her guests as special visitors. Many extra touches make this a home away from home instead of the usual overnight stop. Steaming hot tea and perhaps a wedge of homemade pie will be brought to the room upon request, although many visitors are happiest taking afternoon tea in the lounge by the black marble fireplace. This room is inviting in a casual way with overstuffed chairs, lots of well-worn books and magazines, and

table games for rainy summer days or cool evenings. Mrs. Murphy has a fire going in the fireplace here on cool days.

Grand Harbour Inn was built in 1903 and spent its early years as a tourist home–inn. It became a one-family home in 1912 and remained in that family more than fifty years. In 1974 the house was given a modernizing overhaul, and a new kitchen was installed. The guest rooms retain their old-fashioned period washstands, maple headboards, and handmade quilts. Two share a bath and the others share a hall bath.

The restaurant–dining room, open to guests and to the public for all three meals, serves fresh-fish specialties. Pies come warm from the oven with sharp cheddar cheese or ice cream, hands-down favorite desserts. With two-hours' notice, guests may dine on lobster that has apparently been happily paddling about in the bay only a few hours before.

Accommodations: 5 rooms sharing 2 baths. *Pets:* Allowed "within reason," meaning if they are small and well-behaved. *Driving Instructions:* See Marathon Inn, below, for instructions on how to reach the island. Grand Harbour Inn is 7 miles from the ferry slip.

MARATHON INN

North Head, Grand Manan, New Brunswick. Mailing address: P.O. Box 129, Grand Manan, New Brunswick EOG 2MO, Canada. 506-662-8144. *Innkeepers:* The Leslie family. Open all year.

The Marathon Inn was built in 1871 by a retired sea captain who had enough time on his hands to do the job right. Much of its furniture has been there since the building's construction. Marathon Inn has the high ceilings, tall windows, and hardwood floors typical of the Victorian era. Overlooking the fisherman's wharf, Marathon Inn serves up inviting dinners bought, in many cases, from the fishermen just outside the doorstep. Rooms at the Marathon are usually rented on the Modified American Plan, and dinner guests are given a choice of fresh fish or a meat dish. Typical selections include baked haddock with lemon and mushroom sauce, sautéed scallops, prime ribs, or rock Cornish hens. Meals start with soup and salad and include Fern Leslie's homemade rolls and freshly baked desserts.

Each guest room has running water, and two have parlor stoves and face the ocean. There is a Franklin stove in the living room as well as a library for guests to enjoy. The inn is on 10 landscaped acres, a short walk from the busy harbor and wharfs.

Accommodations: 33 rooms, 5 with private bath. *Driving Instructions:* Grand Manan Island is reached by ferry from Black's Harbor, New Brunswick. Take Route 1 to the Black's Harbor turnoff about 4 miles east of Saint George. The route to the ferry terminal is well marked. The boat journey takes about 1½ hours, and the inn is a short walking distance from the dock.

Rothesay

SHADOW LAWN INN

Rothesay, New Brunswick, Canada. 506-847-7539. *Innkeepers:* Willie and Jean Ward. Open all year.

In 1850 the Prince of Wales, traveling as the Duke of Rothesay, paid a visit to this region just north of Saint John. He was so taken with the spot, he presented it with the name of Rothesay after a village on the Isle of Bate in Scotland. Canada's Rothesay is a quiet village of tree-lined streets and lawns. The Prince would feel quite at home here today, especially at Shadow Lawn, in an 1870 mansion. The inn is surrounded by shade trees, well cared for lawn, and ornamental bushes and green vines. The large white building has several wings, a shady porch, and levels of mansard roofs flanked by tall red chimneys. Guests are ushered in through a glassed-in porch to the spacious entrance hall, where a hearth fire adds a special welcome on chilly days.

Downstairs the drawing room and other public rooms have working fireplaces, as do most of the other public rooms, and are furnished throughout with period antiques. Guests are offered an afternoon sherry in the drawing room, where parties and dances are held throughout the year. Cocktails are available in the Smokeroom Bar, and a small dining room is open to guests and the public by reservation. The Wards offer no posted menu but discuss choices individually with guests. All the seafood dishes and the Wards' beef Wellington rank as favorites with the inn's many devotees. The dining room service is well-appointed with bone china and sterling silver, and the room glows with candlelight from the many silver candelabra.

Guest rooms are in the main house and in a converted barn with three attractive suites. Most of the rooms have working fireplaces; these can be requested when reserving. The inn is renowned for its service in both dining and lodgings.

Visitor attractions are numerous in Rothesay and in the area of Saint John immediately to the south. Rothesay offers tennis, golf, swimming in salt and fresh water, fishing, and sailing on the river. A number of little toll-free ferries criss-cross the river at historic villages and sites. Saint John, Canada's first incorporated city, blossomed overnight into the "Loyalist City" when some three thousand United Empire Loyalists, who preferred to live under the British flag, landed here on May 18, 1783, after England's defeat in her colonies. The

450-mile-long Saint John River, without doubt the biggest attraction around, literally and figuratively, empties into the Bay of Fundy at the narrow mouth to the harbor. Tides at this point measure some 28½ feet. At low tide the waters are 14½ feet below the river level, causing rapids to rush out into the harbor. The direction of the rapids is reversed by the high tide, and this tremendous tidal force is felt as far as 80 miles upstream. For information on the Reversing Tidal Falls and the many historic sights along the Loyalist Trail in Saint John, visitors can go to the Visitors and Convention Bureau at City Hall on Market Square.

Accommodations: 12 rooms, 8 with private bath. *Driving Instructions:* Take Route 100 from Saint John about 8 miles to Rothesay and the inn.

MARSHLANDS INN

73 Bridge Street, Sackville, New Brunswick. Mailing address: P.O. Box 1440, Sackville, New Brunswick EOA 3CO, Canada. 506-536-0170. *Innkeepers:* Herb and Alice Read. Open early February to early December.

Marshlands is an exquisite country inn fashioned out of a fine 1850s home in 1935 by the Herbert W. Read family. Marshlands was built by William Crane for his daughter, whose portrait hangs in the hall. The home was purchased in 1895 by Henry C. Read, who named it Marshlands after the intriguing Tantramar marshes surrounding the town. "Tantramar" comes from the Indian word "Tintamarre," meaning "sound of bird wings," and indeed, the marshes are one of the main flyways of North America. In spring and fall, huge flights of geese and ducks may be seen coming to rest there. An estimated two million birds make the marshes their temporary home during the migratory season. The Reads have been in the stone business since the early nineteenth century, operating quarries in nine locations. Their stone products were used to construct the old city hall and Queen's Point in Toronto and produced grindstones for several generations of craftsmen before synthetic stones replaced the natural products.

Soon after buying Marshlands, Mr. Read made a number of improvements to the structure, adding three rooms to the top front of the house and a large room to the rear. He increased the number of fireplaces throughout his home to a total of seven, added the veranda and sunporch, and enlarged the dining room. The Reads opened their home to the public as an inn in 1935 and it has continued to operate that way ever since. The second generation of Reads are now the innkeepers with hopes that another Read will continue the family tradition.

Marshlands is an inn of great dignity, with excellent workmanship and a tasteful blending of fine woods, period furnishings, and such focal points as a leaded-glass oval window in the dining room and a hand-painted William Morris frieze. Polished sterling silver gleams on tables and sideboards, reflecting the light cast by early electric-lighting fixtures on the walls and ceilings. Throughout the inn, original oil paintings, both portraits and still lifes, add to its nineteenth-century feeling. Each guest room is distinctive. Some are pocket-sized and under the eaves; others, like the huge attic room,

could sleep an entire family. The latter has an elaborately carved four-poster bed whose posts are larger than a man, a double-sleigh bed and a single bed, two loveseats, and Oriental scatter rugs on the hardwood floor.

At Marshlands, an array of food is laid out from morning to evening. Breakfasts include hearty north-country offerings like old-fashioned porridge, creamed salt-cod, kippers, country sausage, ham, or bacon, pancakes, and eggs. The dinner menu starts with haddock chowder or Canadian pea soup and follows with such specialties as baked scallops Marshlands, boiled salt cod with pork scraps, steak and kidney pie, and Miramichi salmon with lemon or egg sauce. Marshlands is a good place to taste your first fiddlehead fern; this specialty of New Brunswick is the young fern frond—before it has unfurled—braised until tender and delicious. Other Marshlands delicacies that you may not have tried elsewhere include rhubarb punch and stewed foxberries and gooseberries. To cap the day, cocoa and homemade gingersnaps are served every evening at 10:00 just before guests retire.

Accommodations: 18 rooms, 8 with private bath. Eight of these rooms are just across the driveway in Hanson House, which has furnishings like those in the main house. *Driving Instructions:* Take the Trans-Canada Highway (Route 2) to exit 541 (Sackville). Route 6 will bring you to the center of town.

THE ALGONQUIN HOTEL

Saint Andrews-by-the-Sea, New Brunswick EOG 2XO, Canada. 506-529-8823. *Innkeeper:* David R. Smith. Open late May to early September.

For those who desire the comforts and services of a 200-room hotel along with the peace and quiet of a seaside vacation, the Algonquin is the answer. This is surely one of the handsomest of the many hotels in the Canadian Pacific Hotel chain. Its brochure touts the hotel as a "gabled storybook mansion," and it lives up to the description. In the summer the lawns outside the hotel are broken by borders of flowering plants and manicured shrubs. The building itself reveals its English heritage with half-timbering above a stone foundation. Its upper floor has more dormers than one can easily count, and towers pierce the roof in several spots. Within, the hotel's summery look is established by pale, cream-colored walls and light-toned fabrics on the chairs and drapes.

Dining at the Algonquin varies from very informal to the seaside elegance of the Passamaquoddy Dining Room. Here the menu reflects the hotel's location overlooking Passamaquoddy Bay with seafood leading the list of specialties for both meal starters and entrees. First courses include such delights as baked seafood in a shell, fresh Fundy seafood cocktail, lobster bisque, or Matane shrimp cocktail. Entrees from the sea include baked haddock, crepe stuffed with seafood Newburg, grilled salmon, or boiled Saint Andrews lobster. As alternatives, the hotel frequently has chicken cordon bleu, roast prime ribs of beef, filet mignon, flamed pepper steak, or chateaubriand. New Brunswick fiddlehead ferns are served all summer long, a specialty of both the inn and the province.

The Algonquin recently underwent a $2.5 million renovation program that has seen each of its guest rooms thoroughly redone. Fine contemporary hotel furnishings, freshly painted walls, and simple decorations are the hallmark of the revitalized hotel. In addition to the usual range of standard rooms, a number of suites consisting of a parlor and one or two bedrooms are available.

Entertainment is offered in Dick Turpin's Pub, a timbered lounge reminiscent of many we have seen in England. There is a new adult

games room with billiards, table tennis, and table-top shuffleboard. Outdoor sports are popular at the hotel with golf on its nine-hole or championship eighteen-hole courses leading the list. There is shuffleboard, tennis on two courts, swimming in the pool or the clear salt waters of Katy's Cove. In the evenings guests frequently gather in the Sunset Lounge with its book-lined shelves, model sailing ships, and nightly entertainment (except on Sunday evenings). Saint Andrews is an attractive town filled with antique, curio, and handicraft shops—a fine place to browse on a rainy day.

Accommodations: 200 rooms with private bath. *Driving Instructions:* From Saint Stephen take Route 1 east for about 9 miles to Route 127, then go south for about 10 miles to Saint Andrews.

ROSSMOUNT INN

R.R. 2, Saint Andrews, New Brunswick EOG 2XO, Canada. 506-529-3351. *Innkeepers:* George and Marion Brewin. Open May to October.

The Rossmount Inn, on a hill at the foot of Chamcook Mountain, is a quiet retreat and proof that a gracious way of life remarkably still exists. The 87-acre estate encompasses the mountain, the highest point in the Passamaquoddy Bay area. The Brewins have set aside 65 of these acres as a private wildlife preserve, and guests often glimpse wild deer feeding in the meadows and orchard. The inn, built in 1783, welcomed travelers from the very beginning. The Brewins are devoted Anglophiles, and the museum-like inn reveals this passion in every nook and cranny. It has soft-hued Oriental rugs, fine polished woods in all public and guest-room furnishings and woodwork, sterling-silver accessories, and warm colors cast by the sunlight through stained-glass windows. Guests immediately feel the opulence as they enter the large reception hall: A crystal chandelier reflects in the mirrors of the many Victorian pieces; the coronation chair used by the King of Belgium at the coronation of Queen Elizabeth II graces the hall. Antiques throughout the inn are primarily formal Victorian and unmistakably British. A private bar, for the use of guests and dining patrons only, features a piano originally intended for Kaiser Wilhelm, until World War I diverted it here. A bay window comprised of three early stained-glass windows, which once graced an eighteenth-century English chapel, now adds its glow to the dining room. Each window depicts the motto and symbols of the three crowns of Great Britain: the rose of England, the thistle of Scotland, and the harp of Ireland.

The cuisine and impeccable service at the Rossmount have received much national and international acclaim. Specialties are the fish and lobster fresh from Passamaquoddy Bay and the well-aged, prime grass-fed beef. A favorite soup is cream of fiddlehead, a specialty of the province. All breads, pastries, soups and chowders, and sauces are made from scratch in the inn's kitchen, and the vegetables, in season, come straight from the Brewins' own garden.

An imposing staircase guarded by Shakespeare himself leads to the guest rooms, which are furnished with antiques from all over the world. Hallways feature Victorian sitting areas with views of the bay and Minister's Island. The Rossmount has been host to one president of the United States and two Canadian prime ministers. Many visiting government and state officials are frequent guests.

A favorite recreation is the hike to the top of Chamcook Moun-

tain. Its summit offers 360-degree panoramic views of Maine, the coastline, the bay and its islands, and the famous Bar Road, which disappears under the Bay of Fundy tides. Saint Andrews, with its many little shops, two golf courses, and fishing, is just minutes from the inn. The Rossmount estate provides a heated swimming pool, skiing, jogging and nature trails, and scenic hiking.

Accommodations: 18 guest rooms with private bath. *Pets:* Not permitted. *Driving Instructions:* From Saint Stephen, about 16 miles away, take Route 1 to Route 127 and follow signs to Saint Andrews and the inn. From Saint John, about 70 miles away, take Route 1 to Route 127 and follow signs.

SHIRETOWN INN

Town Square, Saint Andrews-by-the-Sea, New Brunswick. Mailing address: P.O. Box 145, Saint Andrews-by-the-Sea, New Brunswick EOG 2XO, Canada. 506-529-8877. *Innkeepers:* Ian and Leni MacKay. Open all year.

For years, Saint Andrews-by-the-Sea has attracted thousands of vacationers from Canada and the United States to its historic shores on Passamaquoddy Bay. Franklin D. Roosevelt was one of the most prominent summer residents of the area, and his estate on nearby Campobello Island is now an international park. Roosevelt once stayed overnight at a little hotel on Saint Andrews's town square. The place was the Shiretown Inn, built in 1881. During its construction the carpenters and laborers received 90 cents for their ten-hour day. The moment the roof and walls were up, the bar was opened; any workman not spending part of his pay at that bar was immediately fired. Presumably they did a good job in spite of the working conditions, and the inn is still thriving today.

The white clapboard hotel stands at curbside and has a two-story veranda and a rooftop widow's walk. In summer the porch is transformed into a sidewalk café overlooking the square. Just beyond the square is the Saint Andrews's wharf, where the world-famous Bay of Fundy tides can be observed to rise and fall some 25 feet or more daily. The Shiretown serves meals every day to guests and public in three old-fashioned dining rooms, each featuring fresh local seafood. Even the breakfast buffet has a fish entree. These rooms have been decorated around a particular theme. The bar is a rustic old-English-style pub with exposed beams and a woodburning stove on a brick hearth next to a bar painted red. The tea room is light and airy, and the main dining room is colonial, with gold accents, white wooden wainscoting beneath small-print wallpaper, chandeliers, and a hutch displaying collections of antique china.

The inn's guest rooms have been modernized with wall-to-wall carpeting and private baths. Most are still furnished with the old-fashioned original dressers, beds, and chairs.

The Shiretown's innkeeper, Ian MacKay, also operates the nearby Smuggler's Wharf, which houses waterside dining rooms and a bar. This building has been extensively remodeled and contains several fully equipped apartments for guests. These rooms feature exposed beams and modern furnishings and are rented by either the week or the day. Several suites have harbor views, as do the dining rooms below. The Wharf has been around since the 1840s and was first used as a wine-and-spirits warehouse. Saint Andrews's first bank robbery took place here. These guest rooms can be booked through the Shiretown Inn.

There is much to do in Saint Andrews and its environs. The town offers walking tours of many of the public buildings and some of the old homes. Cruises of the Fundy Islands are available at the main wharf. Salt-water swimming, tennis, and a boat-launching ramp are provided at Katy's Cove, and in winter there is excellent ice skating, as well as cross-country skiing and curling in the area. Two nearby golf courses are open to the public. The Sunbury Shores Arts and Nature Center on Water Street offers scheduled guided walks exploring tidal pools and other features of the tidal phenomena that make the Saint Andrews region unique. The Saint Andrews Tourist Bureau in town can direct visitors to local historic and sightseeing attractions.

Accommodations: 20 rooms with private bath. Other lodgings available in Smuggler's Wharf. *Driving Instructions:* Saint Andrews-by-the-Sea is on Route 127 off Route 1. The Shiretown Inn is on the town square.

Saint Stephen

ELM LODGE INN

477 Milltown Boulevard, Milltown Heights, Saint Stephen, New Brunswick EOG 2KO, Canada. 506-466-3771. *Innkeepers:* Patrick and Zena Garbutt. Open all year.

The Elm Lodge is what travelers wish for when they go off exploring bumpy country roads: a Victorian country inn with a large canopied bed, plenty of good English food, and at least six hearths aglow with log fires. Take all this, add two terrific innkeepers and a small country town, and you have Elm Lodge Inn. Pat and Zena Garbutt restored their Willow Place Inn in Como, Province of Quebec (which see), and then sold it in order to devote all their time and energies to the Elm Lodge. The inn has been painstakingly restored to its former standing as a country estate of the mid-nineteenth century. Fireplaces were opened up, floors sanded, rooms papered with appropriate period wallcoverings and decorated with Canadian antiques and art gathered in forays into the Quebec and New Brunswick countrysides. All this effort has led Pat Garbutt to insist that the "most battered antique here is the innkeeper himself."

Today the inn invites guests to bask in the warmth of the dining room hearth and the glow from the many antique oil lamps that are lit each evening without fail. Meals are served in four intimate dining rooms, two with working fireplaces. A typical meal might begin with a creamy fish chowder, proceed to a steak and kidney pie or a crisp duckling with orange sauce, and be topped off with a walnut raisin pie or English trifle. Cocktails are offered in the fireside bar. If a guest is still chilly—then off to bed in one of the three antique-filled bedrooms featuring a working fireplace. The Honeymoon Suite has one of the biggest four-poster canopied beds anywhere. It was rescued in a decrepit state from a barn where it had spent some fifteen years, and a cabinetmaker friend of the innkeepers' restored it.

The Elm Lodge Inn is truly international, standing just 50 yards from the United States–Canadian border within view of the Canadian customs house. The inn is flanked by lovely wineglass-shaped elms and well-cared-for flower gardens. Milltown Heights in Saint Stephen, just across the Saint Croix River from Maine, is an old-fashioned place with tree-lined streets. There is much to occupy visitors, such as horseback riding, canoeing, sailing, bicycling, and hiking. The Oak Bay Provincial Park is nearby, and the inn is an ideal base for day trips to the Fundy Islands and surrounding historic towns. One can even get to Campobello Island from here on a day trip.

Accommodations: 9 rooms, 5 with private bath. *Pets and Children:* Permitted if very well-behaved. *Driving Instructions:* From Saint John, New Brunswick, take Route 1. From Bangor, Maine, take Route 9 across the Milltown-Calais and Milltown-Saint Stephen International Border Crossing. The inn is within sight of the customs house.

Newfoundland

THE VILLAGE INN

Trinity, Trinity Bay, Newfoundland AOC 2SO, Canada. 709-464-3269. *Innkeepers:* Peter and Chris Beamish. Open all year, by reservation.

We confess that our investigation of Newfoundland is only in its infancy, but when we heard of the Village Inn and historic Trinity, we could not resist investigating. Newfoundland's tourism is, in many respects, in its own infancy. Traditionally a land of seafaring people, the province is just beginning to capitalize on its many attractions that are truly not available elsewhere. Certainly the Village Inn is the essence of this approach: Take the very best of local cuisine and combine it (in the summer months) with a vacation experience that one can not have at any other inn in North America, and you have a formula for certain success.

Peter Beamish holds his doctorate in studies of the cetacean (whale and dolphin) family. Every summer his company, known as Ocean Contact, Ltd., holds special one-week expeditions in which the goal is human-cetacean contact. By contact, Peter means communication with these gentle animals through sight, low-frequency sound, and possibly even touch. Every day the small group of expedition members ventures into the local bays of eastern Newfoundland during the summer cetacean-feeding season. Using small boats, they

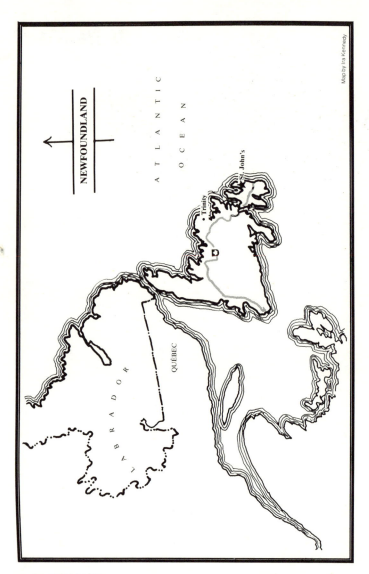

NEWFOUNDLAND

ATLANTIC OCEAN

St. John's

Trinity

QUÉBEC

LABRADOR

Map by Ira Kennedy

come as close as possible to these animals, which range in size from small dolphins to mature humpback whales. The expedition uses the Village Inn owned by the Beamishes as its home base. The inn is open all year; in summer, when inn rooms rapidly fill with expedition members, the Beamishes will make every attempt to place prospective guests either in available rooms at the inn or in local homes.

The Village Inn is a two-story white clapboard structure originally built as a hotel by the Canadian Pacific Railway but never actually operated by them. Over the years it served as a two-family dwelling and a grocery store–tavern. The eighty-year-old building was renovated four years ago for use as an inn. There are five guest rooms upstairs with iron bedsteads covered with locally made quilts. Antique washstands and dressers complement the furniture. Some rooms have barnboard on the walls, others use old-fashioned wallpapers.

The Spouter Pub downstairs is popular with guests and local people alike. Dark stained wainscoting, salvaged from the hotel's former third floor, which was demolished in the renovations, is now on all the room's walls. A brick fireplace, its ornate mantel complete with imprinted figurines, is centered on one wall. Across from the pub is the inn's dining room, seating only two dozen diners at a time. It is formally set with white linen cloths, and one's attention is immediately drawn to the intricately carved 5-foot mahogany blue whale, a gift to the Beamishes by California carver Leo Jacobson. Formal Victorian wallpapers over waist-high wainscoting add to the tone of the room. The Beamishes have established what may be the foremost Newfoundland kitchen exclusively offering the cuisine unique to the province. Peter has a particular rule that all fish served must be caught in the past twenty-four hours (it is delivered daily just before noon) and never frozen. As one might expect, seafood dominates the changing menu. Guests and the public are offered a meal of the day, with no choices. However, especially for guests registered in the cetacean program, this turns out to be virtually of banquet proportions. Typical entrees include baked local salmon, fresh fried cod with pork scrunchions (crisp pork bits), Newfoundland rabbit, cod tongues and cheeks, local lobster, and the special Jiggs Dinner, named for its popularity with fishermen who come back hungry from a long day of jigging codfish. It includes salt beef, cabbage, pease pudding (shades of the nursery rhyme), carrots, turnips, and potatoes. Popular starters are cod au gratin, local snails, sea urchin roe (the Japanese call it *uni*), capelin roe (now recognized as a major new caviar), and partridge berry salad. The latter, berries of the wintergreen plant, find their way onto the Village Inn tables frequently. They are often served as jam for breakfast, as a sauce on ice cream, or baked in pies for dinner. An unusual appetizer, especially popular with locals, is codfish and brewis, a stewlike dish combining brewis—a kind of hardtack or dried bread—with cod, fried scrunchions, and onions. The banquets served to guests registered for the whale-contact experiences often include formal butler service, fine California wines, and an evening slide-presentation following dinner.

Accommodations: 5 rooms sharing 2 baths. *Driving Instructions:* Take Route 1 to Clarenville, then Route 230 north, and finally Route 239 to Trinity.

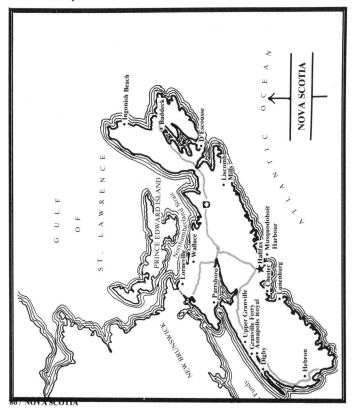

Nova Scotia

Annapolis Royal

BREAD AND ROSES

82 Victoria Street, Annapolis Royal, Nova Scotia. Mailing address: P.O. Box 177, Annapolis Royal, Nova Scotia BOS 1AO, Canada. 902-532-5727. *Innkeepers:* John and Barbara Taylor.

Open mid-May to mid-October; other times by arrangement only. The Annapolis Basin area of Nova Scotia can be considered the cradle of Canada. In 1605, under the direction of Samuel Champlain, French Acadian pioneers constructed l'Habitation de Port Royal not far from the present town of Annapolis Royal. This was the first permanent European settlement north of Saint Augustine, Florida. Today, Annapolis Royal is the hub of the Evangeline district, a town filled with museums and old homes.

Our vote for the best place to stay here is a bed-and-breakfast inn known as Bread and Roses. The Taylors explain the origin of the inn's intriguing name in their brochure: ''Bread and Roses takes its name from the poem by James Oppenheim written in 1912 in response to the women textile workers' strike in Lawrence, Massachusetts, seeking a reduction from a 56- to a 54-hour workweek without loss of pay. The marching women carried a banner saying 'We want bread and roses, too.' Bread and Roses is dedicated to the concept that people require not only the basic essentials in life, but beauty and inspiration as well.''

Bread and Roses is a restored Victorian mansion constructed by Italian craftsmen in 1885 in the Gothic Revival tradition. It was ordered built by a flamboyant dentist who wished to upstage the local doctor. The size of the rooms in the large brick structure is in proportion to the impression the dentist wanted to make. As you enter Bread and Roses, you are confronted with a central hallway paneled with fine woods and a wide paneled staircase lighted by a large lamp salvaged from a demolished Toronto church. Dr. Cunningham, the first owner, clearly appreciated the richness of fine woods. Rather than select just one or two for his home, he used black cherry, black walnut, Honduras mahogany, oak, ash, and tiger maple, and he often combined two side by side for contrast.

Each of the spacious guest rooms at Bread and Roses has been furnished with antique pieces gleaned from local dealers and yard sales. Two of the bedrooms have their own fireplaces (although fires are not permitted), and all have private baths. Two bathrooms contain the original fixtures; those in the rest were added during the Taylors' renovation. Downstairs are the parlor, dining room, and library. The first two rooms contain tiled fireplaces, large bay windows, and local paintings and crafts, some of which are offered for sale by the Taylors. Bread and Roses remains pleasantly cool in the summer thanks to the thick brick walls and 11-foot ceilings. In consideration of many of their guests, the Taylors do not permit smoking in the public rooms.

Breakfast at Bread and Roses may be chosen from an à la carte menu offering choices of a Continental meal, a cereal breakfast, or a complete egg breakfast. Prices vary accordingly. The Taylors have recently started offering an evening meal to guests and the public on Wednesday through Saturday evenings, with a single sitting at 7 P.M. John and Barbara are vegetarians, and their new menus reflect this. They offer organically grown vegetables and fruit from their own garden in season. Each dinner is focused on a particular ethnic cuisine. Their Italian dinner starts with antipasto and garlic bread, continues with zucchini fritti and lasagna, and ends with cappuccino. Their Nova Scotian dinner includes split-pea soup, brown bread, whole-wheat macaroni and cheese, honeyed carrots, cole slaw, pickles, homemade sherbet, and tea or coffee.

Accommodations: 7 rooms with private bath. *Pets:* Permitted if well-behaved. *Driving Instructions:* Take Route 1 to Annapolis Royal. The inn is behind Saint Luke's Anglican Church.

MILFORD HOUSE

South Milford, R.R. 4, Annapolis Royal, Nova Scotia B0S 1A0, Canada. 902-532-2617. *Innkeeper:* Warren J. Miller. Open June 15 to September 15.

Milford House is a complex of woodland and lakeside cottages around a main lodge in an unspoiled 600-acre preserve of woods, lakes, and streams. Milford House, an early stopping place for coaches and travelers beginning in the 1860s, bore several names down through the years: Half-Way House, Thomas Hotel, and finally, Milford House. It has attracted families and sportsmen, many of whom owned the individual rustic cabins. They came to enjoy the peace and quiet, the pleasures of canoeing on pristine lakes, trout fishing, moose hunting, or just sitting by the fireside. In 1969 a group of devoted guests formed a company, known as the Milford House Properties Ltd., dedicated to operating the house and the cottages in the same simple way while preserving the scenic beauty of the property.

The main lodge, a rambling white building, is the focal point of the operation. It is surrounded by lawns and gardens, croquet grounds, and a tennis court. Guests gather here to visit or just relax in the comfort of the old-fashioned, parlor-like lounges. The rooms are furnished with plenty of country antiques, old rugs, and such touches as Regulator clocks on the mantels or a moosehead or two presiding over a corner niche. The lodge contains a well-stocked library, game room, and a large country dining room where guests and the public can enjoy hearty cooking. It offers enormous farm-kitchen breakfasts and dinners, the kind that bring people back year after year. Everything is fresh—fish, homemade breads, rolls, and pastries, local blueberries and raspberries, and plenty of vegetables from the garden outside. Breakfasts feature just about everything one could ask for, with an occasional treat like pan-fried trout or blueberry muffins.

Guests stay in rustic cottages that are within walking distance of the lodge. Situated along the wooded shore but well-screened from each other, the cottages come with their own lake jetties for tying up canoes, which can be leased from Milford House by the day or week. No motors are allowed to spoil the tranquility of this retreat. The lodge supplies the cottages with maid service and very limited cooking facilities. Each cabin has a living room with an old stone fireplace and a supply of firewood, a bathroom, and a minimum of two bedrooms. The stamp of former owners remains in the cabins: old postcards, souvenirs, old mystery novels on bookshelves, and even a family portrait or two. The wind in the trees, the slap of a beaver's tail, the quacking of the wild ducks, or a fleeting glimpse of a deer's white tail as it bounds off—all contribute to this pleasant setting.

Accommodations: 25 cottages with bath (65 bedrooms in all).
Driving Instructions: Milford House is 15 miles from Annapolis Royal on Route 8.

Baddeck

INVERARY INN

P.O. Box 190, Baddeck, Cape Breton, Nova Scotia BOE 1BO, Canada. 902-295-2674. *Innkeeper:* Isobel MacAulay. Open May through October.

The Inverary Inn began life as an 11-acre farm at the edge of Bras d'Or Lakes some 150 years ago. The farmhouse was built by a local fellow, "Millionaire MacNeil," who amassed a fortune in Boston and returned home to impress his countrymen. The farm stood deserted for a number of years, and the land returned to its natural state. Today, shady paths wind through the woods to the private bathing wharf on the lakes. The present inn has been extensively modernized, and several sections have been added. It is famed far and wide for the Scottish fare served in its large dining room, which has walls of windows overlooking the water, cupboards filled with china, and pots of plants. One can view the highlands from the windows: Beinn Bhreagh Mountain, which Alexander Graham Bell and his wife loved so dearly. The popular breakfasts at the inn include spiced apple-sauce, Scottish oatcakes and oatmeal topped with thick fresh cream, bannock (Scottish griddlecakes), and Mharagh with home fries (ask about it).

Mrs. MacAulay and her son, who manage the inn, put guests immediately at ease. The warmth and strong overtones of the Scottish highlands are evident from the start. The rooms have colorful tartan draperies at the windows. Guests may relax by the stone hearth in the paneled living room. The comfortable rooms are modernized, many with private baths and knotty-pine paneling. The cottages are often preferred by families. The complex of buildings includes the old farmhouse with its additions, the barn, wagon house, and cottages, all situated amid the wildflowers and grasses of this town. Baddeck was settled by Highlanders from Scotland, and the culture is well preserved. In summer the Highland Village Society of Iona and the Gaelic College of Saint Ann's hold outdoor concerts featuring highland dances, songs, and bagpipe music. Baddeck, with its clear waters and sheltered harbors, is a good spot for boating enthusiasts. Lovers of Scottish foods will find the Inverary Inn an ideal stopover.

Accommodations: 62 rooms, 54 with private bath. Some rooms are in cottages and modern lodges. Be sure to specify when reserving. *Pets:* Not permitted. *Driving Instructions:* Take the first exit off the Trans-Canada Highway to Baddeck on Shore Road.

SHEET ANCHOR HOUSE

Corner of South and Central streets, Chester, Nova Scotia. Mailing address: P.O. Box 395, Chester, Nova Scotia B0J 1J0, Canada. Off-season: 5559 Carriageway Crs., Halifax, Nova Scotia B3K 5K4, Canada. 902-275-4832. *Innkeeper:* Marilyn Janigan. Open June through September.

Sheet Anchor House is a historic early Nova Scotia home overlooking the waters of the Chester Basin. It was built around 1784 by Nathan Levy, who is said to have brought his materials over from New England. One later addition provides needed extra space. The rooms are paneled throughout with pine. An especially attractive piece is the old pine cupboard in the living room. The inn is furnished with local country antiques, mostly of pine. Antique prints decorate the walls and help maintain the old-world atmosphere in keeping with the age of the house. Fires are kept going in the fireplace hearth on chilly spring and fall days.

There are just three attractive little guest rooms at the Sheet Anchor House. A full island breakfast is offered to guests. The seaside town of Chester has several good seafood restaurants for other meals. One, the Sword and Anchor, was until recently part of the complex including the Sheet Anchor House. It, too, is a historic building with views of the harbor. The town has long been the summer home of many wealthy Americans who still maintain summer estates here. A pleasant day's outing would be to go on the pedestrian's ferry from Chester to Big Tancook Island, famed for its oxcart rides, deep-sea fishing, and sauerkraut and corned beef dinners.

Accommodations: 3 rooms with private bath. *Pets:* Not permitted. *Driving Instructions:* The inn is off Route 103, via exit 7 or 8. It is on the corner of South and Central streets by the water.

LENNOX PASSAGE GUEST HOUSE

D'Escousse, Isle Madame, Cape Breton, Nova Scotia BOE 1KO, Canada. 902-226-2349. *Innkeepers:* William and Alida Wicks. Open May 15 through October 15.

This sea captain's home, built in 1870, overlooks Lennox Passage, which runs from the Atlantic to Port Hawkesbury. It also looks out over the Saint Peter's Canal and locks to the Bras d'Or Lakes. The inn is on the Isle Madame, a pastoral island, and its property slopes down to the D'Escousse harbor, which is deep enough and sheltered enough to accommodate oceangoing sloops and yachts. The house is a gingerbread Victorian, its main gable decorated with wooden curls, its roof topped by pointed lightning rods.

Alida and William Wicks offer guests a warm, welcoming atmosphere and plenty of lively conversation. They have made Cape Breton their home for more than twenty years and have explored every inch of it. They are the best sources of information on the area and its scenic farmlands and sheltered harbors. If guests so desire, the Wickses will serve them dinner. These meals feature such local dishes as fresh fish and chowders as well as homebaked pies and rolls. In berry seaon, the pies and muffins are special. Breakfasts at any time of the year offer berries in the form of jams and jellies put up by Mrs.Wicks from the abundant supplies growing in surrounding fields. Meals are served only to guests.

After breakfast the island beckons with its many natural attractions. Hiking and biking trails are excellent. A provincial park 4 miles away offers swimming, picnicking, and golf. At the height of the tourist season, the villages put on outdoor festivities, such as bagpipers and Scottish fiddlers. There are numerous church suppers and displays of island crafts. And, of course, the sea is an endless source of enjoyment.

Accommodations: 4 rooms sharing baths. *Pets:* Not permitted. *Driving Instructions:* The guest house is on Route 320 in the center of D'Escousse on the water side.

THE PINES RESORT HOTEL

Digby, Nova Scotia B0V 1A0, Canada. Winter address: The Pines Resort Hotel, Department of Tourism, P.O. Box 456, Halifax, Nova Scotia B3J 2R5, Canada. Summer phone: 902-245-2511; winter phone: 902-424-3259. *Innkeeper:* The Province of Nova Scotia, Department of Tourism. Open May to mid-October.

The Pines, a large resort in Digby overlooking the Annapolis Basin, is a stone and cement castle of French Norman architecture in a 300-acre setting of landscaped lawns, flower gardens, and woodlands. A green copper dome tops its round stone turret.

The first hotel, Digby Pines, was built on this spot in 1903 by a Mr. Harry Churchill. He retired ten years later, and the hotel spent the ensuing war years as officers' quarters. The Canadian Pacific bought the hotel in 1919 and ten years later ripped it down and built the present edifice. The Province of Nova Scotia, which became the hotel's owner in 1965, renamed it The Pines. Today, its accommodations include hotel guest rooms and nearby modern cottages that have verandas overlooking the lawns, woods, or sea, fully carpeted living rooms, and large stone fireplaces that the management maintains and supplies with firewood. Guest rooms in the main building's three floors have views of the countryside, town, and sea, and are furnished in a traditional manner with twin beds and private baths.

Morning coffee and afternoon tea are served on the large veranda just off the Edna Stark reading room–lounge. The veranda offers panoramas of the inlets, Annapolis Basin, and the village. In addition to coffee and tea, the menu offers little sandwiches and a variety of freshly baked pastries from the hotel's bakery. The Annapolis Room, the hotel's restaurant–dining room, overlooks the lawns and gardens and offers a menu of traditional and imaginative dishes to please a wide range of palates as well as domestic wines to accompany dinners. The Good Times Lounge offers cocktails and features live music for listening and dancing.

The Pines is a genuine seaside resort providing many recreational and sightseeing opportunities. Just in front of the hotel is a large heated pool, secluded sunbathing area, shuffleboard courts, and a putting green. The newly surfaced tennis courts, lighted for night games, are across the road and down by the waterside where players are cooled by the fresh sea breezes. The coast beckons visitors to stroll the rocky shores and observe the local fishermen at their weirs and the scallop fleet. The famous tides can be seen from the hotel. The average range of tidal heights is about 32 feet twice daily; in the full moon of the spring tides can reach as high as 50 feet. About ½ mile away is The Pines's championship eighteen-hole golf course and clubhouse. Other offerings include a fitness jogging trail, children's play areas, and the services of a full-time social director, who assists in organizing such excursions as fresh- and salt-water fishing, scalloping, sailing charters, airplane excursions, and tours of historic areas as well as nighttime activities like Bingo and movies.

Accommodations: 96 hotel rooms and 30 cottages, each with 1 to 3 bedrooms. *Pets:* Inquire before bringing. *Driving Instructions:* The hotel is north of Digby on Road No. 217 off Route 101/1. It is well marked.

Granville Ferry

THE MOORINGS

P.O. Box 47, Granville Ferry, Nova Scotia BOS IKO, Canada. 902-532-2146. *Innkeepers:* Vina and Bill Percy. Open June through September.

The Moorings is a peaceful inn surrounded by many historic homes. It was built by Captain Joseph Hall in the days of the sailing ships, near the end of the nineteenth century. The large white waterfront home looks out over the sparkling water toward historic Fort Anne and Annapolis Royal, Canada's oldest town. Just outside the door of The Moorings, the tide rises and falls 28 feet twice daily. Large merchant ships make their way to the wharf across the way, only to be left high and dry by the receding tides.

Guests are made to feel welcome even before walking through the inn's door. Its green lawn is set off by flower beds, and the inviting veranda has summer chairs and hanging baskets of flowers joined by a flowering clematis or two. Behind the inn is a large carriage house, its weathered timber creating fascinating patterns in the sunlight.

The large entrance hall opens onto a Victorian parlor with period furnishings: red velvet drapes, a black marble fireplace, and oil lamps. On the other side of the hall is a library-lounge where guests can read or watch the inn's only television. This room contains a carved oak fireplace with a whole stage-setting in the cast-iron firebacks. The Grecian ladies portrayed here seem to dance in the firelight; the Percys make sure a fire is always alight. All the rooms and the hallways have the original decorative metal ceilings and ornate plasterwork in prime condition. The fine woodwork, ceilings, and fireplaces throughout the house work to create an atmosphere of days gone by.

The spacious guest rooms feature seating areas by large windows overlooking the water and have Victorian furnishings with good beds and comfortable armchairs. The family room has a double bed and two singles; the other two have a double bed and two singles respectively. Two bathrooms serve the guests, one with a modern shower and tub and the other with the original marble sink and deep, clawfooted tub.

Vina and Bill Percy offer guests breakfast in the dining room amid more Victoriana. Dinner is served only to guests, at their request—and guests would be well advised to make that request! Meals feature seafood fresh out of the local waters: sole, haddock, and scallops. Another of the Percys' specialties is a steak and kidney pie. The vegetables are all home grown; fresh fruits, in season, include raspberries, strawberries, peaches, and apples, all served up in pies and short-cakes.

The Granville Ferry area is steeped in history, so much so that several ghost sightings have been reported. Local people insist that The Moorings has its very own ghost, that of an unhappy young girl who was born and died here. The previous owner believes to have seen her, but the Percys have not as yet had the pleasure and feel that she has probably moved on. Who knows? Come find out for yourself.

Accommodations: 3 rooms, sharing 2 bathrooms. *Pets:* Not permitted. *Driving Instructions:* A causeway joins Granville Ferry with Annapolis Royal.

Hebron

THE MANOR INN

P.O. Box 56, Yarmouth County, Nova Scotia BOW 1XO, Canada. 902-742-7841. *Innkeeper:* John Miller. Open all year.

The Manor Inn was built early in the twentieth century in colonial style. The white clapboard house has dark shutters, many levels, roof peaks dotted with large chimneys, and an imposing patio entrance-way. The inn was once the estate of a Commodore H. H. Raymond, who retired here to live graciously among his fellow countrymen after "making good" in the big city. The Manor stands on four acres of flowerbeds, ornamental bushes, and trees on Doctor's Lake. The Commodore had his own private stock of trout in the estate's stream, which runs down to the Manor's half-mile of lake frontage. The centerpiece of the well-cared-for landscaping is an enclosed circular rose garden of more than two hundred prize hybrid tea roses.

The interior woodwork in the main house is noted for its beauty;

the staircase is of South American mahogany. The bar and two dining rooms have working fireplaces decorated with Wedgwood carved mantelpieces. One of the dining rooms and the English bar overlook the rose garden. The menu at Manor Inn's Commodore Restaurant features lobster, prime roast beef, and home-baked pies. Innkeeper John Miller has set up an additional cocktail lounge in a concealed part of the house where the Commodore kept his whiskey still and served guests during Prohibition. The extensive cocktail lounge and restaurant facilities are popular with vacationers. There is nightly entertainment with music and dancing in the lounge and even a discotheque.

Guest accommodations in the main house have been revamped with private baths and decorator-designed and -furnished rooms. Two have working fireplaces; all have cable television and private telephones. Six rooms are in the Manor; the rest are housed in the new modern structure adjacent to the rose garden overlooking the lake.

Yarmouth County is at the western tip of Nova Scotia. The Historical Museum and a Firefighter Museum contain items of local interest. Swimming is good at nearby beaches and at Lake Ellenwood Park. Port Maitland is excellent for boating and deep-sea fishing enthusiasts. The area abounds with fields of wildflowers and berries in season, and the villages hold weekly flea markets during the summer.

Accommodations: 29 rooms with private bath. *Driving Instructions:* From Yarmouth, go 4 miles north on Route 1, the old highway.

KELTIC LODGE

Ingonish Beach, Nova Scotia BOC 1LO. Off season: P.O. Box 456, Halifax, Nova Scotia B3J 2R5, Canada. 902-285-2880. Off season: 902-424-3258. *Innkeeper:* Roland J. Ziegenfuss. Open June 1 to late October and mid-December to April.

The explorer John Cabot first spotted the shores of Cape Breton Island in 1497, and his name has been given to the trail that circumscribes the island's northern half, for the most part hugging the rugged coastline. About halfway between Baddeck (stop for a visit to the Alexander Graham Bell Museum there) and the northern tip of the island is Ingonish Beach and its world-famous resort at Keltic Lodge. The lodge stands near the edge of the cliffs, overlooking the ocean in front and the bay behind. It has white twin gabled ends connected by a lower, red-roofed section bisected by a pair of matching chimneys that rise high here and at the ends of the lodge.

Keltic Lodge stands on the spot once occupied by the Corson estate. The Henry Corsons of Akron, Ohio, set out at the end of the nineteenth century to find an environment with clean, fresh air for Mrs. Corson, who was suffering from tuberculosis. While on a tour of Cape Breton the couple paused to admire the view from the top of Cape Smokey and across the bay noticed a piece of land thrusting out into the ocean. They immediately bought the property and built their country home. This log structure stood where the main lodge now stands, and there are reminders of the Corsons everywhere. The apple, cherry, and flowering trees were planted by them, and the golf clubhouse was made from the old Corson stables.

Keltic Lodge today is a year-round resort. Best known for its active summer program, it overlooks the Ingonish sandy beach. There is a saltwater swimming pool on the lodge property and a nearby freshwater lake. Ingonish Beach is the gateway to the Cape Breton Highlands National Park, and the park's eighteen-hole golf course is available for guests' use. Other lodge activities include tennis on the nearby park courts, shuffleboard, deep-sea and freshwater fishing, hiking on miles of nearby trails, and sunbathing on the grounds or beachfront.

Keltic Lodge recently opened its doors in winter for the first time.

Just across the bay is the full-service Cape Smokey Ski Area, where a 4,000-foot chairlift services three runs ranging in length from just under to just over a mile. Other Keltic Lodge winter events include sleighrides, tobogganing, ice skating on Warren Lake, ice fishing, and exploring winter nature trails.

Thirty-two guest rooms are available in the main lodge, others in a modern motel unit and in a number of individual cottages. The lodge rooms are traditional in decor with carpeted floors, painted walls, and old-fashioned hotel desks, chairs, and twin beds. The public rooms are characterized by polished hardwood and carpeted floors and painted columns rising to the tall ceilings. The dining room enjoys a fine view of the sea from its picture windows. Luncheons and dinners follow the same format and are available to the public as well as to resident guests. The limited menus always include about four appetizers (typical would be a fresh salad, iced melon, a pâté, or juice) followed by one of three soups and a choice of more than a half-dozen entrees. Recent entree offerings included poulet basquaise, Bouchée à la reine, seafood au gratin, omelett aux épinards, pan-fried scallops, grilled salmon, and sirloin steak with béarnaise sauce.

Accommodations: 96 rooms with private bath. *Driving Instructions:* Take the Cape Breton Trail north from Baddeck to Ingonish Beach. North of the town, follow the signs to Keltic Lodge.

Liscomb Mills

LISCOMBE LODGE

Liscomb Mills, Nova Scotia B0J 2A0, Canada. Off season: Liscombe Lodge, P.O. Box 456, Halifax, Nova Scotia B3J 2R5, Canada. 902-779-2307. *Innkeeper:* David M. Evans, Manager. Open June 1 to October 15.

One of the nicest things about setting out for Liscombe Lodge is the drive from Halifax to Liscomb Mills along Route 7, the Marine Drive. The journey will take you past dozens of small fishing villages that hug some of the finest unspoiled coastline in Nova Scotia. All too often we have rushed past beautiful scenery and historic sites in our rush to get out onto Cape Breton Island. Liscomb Lodge gives one a chance to stop and enjoy a very special part of the coast. It is on a wooded property overlooking the Liscomb River, just below the falls at Liscomb Mills.

Fifteen chalets and five four-bedroom cottages surround the main lodge. Of fairly recent vintage (the earliest chalet was built in 1966), the lodge complex is owned by the province and operated by its department of tourism. The lodge is a perfect base for enjoying Sherbrooke Village, 15 miles away. The village is a restoration of the mid-nineteenth century town that prospered here for about twenty years following the discovery of gold in 1869. As in many other restoration projects, a number of the early trades buildings are once again being operated to produce nineteenth-century-style crafts.

Each of the chalet's and cottages stands surrounded by pines in its own tiny clearing along the Liscombe River. The verandas face the river waters flowing over the stones below. Each chalet has a large bed-sitting room with a fireplace, bath, radio, and its own heat. Each cottage has four twin-bedded rooms with private bath and a common living room with open fireplace. The cottages were furnished with Nova Scotia pine furniture, bedspreads and drapes woven by a Nova Scotia company especially for the lodge, sketches and photos by local artists, and fireplace pieces made at the Sherbrooke Village blacksmith shop. The fireplaces in the chalets and the cottage living rooms are set each morning by the lodge staff.

A fire awaits guests every morning in the dining room hearth at breakfast time and again at lunch and dinner. Meals at the lodge are served à la carte. The luncheon-dinner menu includes Nova Scotia lobster, Atlantic salmon, seafood creole, fillet of halibut, and a number of steaks, chops, chicken, and omelet items. There are also several lighter sandwich and salad plates for luncheon or lighter appetites.

Salmon and trout fishing are major activities at Liscombe Lodge, and the staff will be happy to arrange for guides. There are four excellent salmon rivers nearby, and appropriate equipment is always set up at the lodge so guests can tie their own flies. The lodge maintains its own marina on the Liscombe River; guests who are traveling the Nova Scotia coastline may arrive by boat if they wish. The marina rents paddle boats, canoes, rowboats, and motor boats. There are hiking trails from the lodge to suit all tastes, including a nature trail and a fitness trail. Guests walking down to the marina may be able to identify the site of a cabin once occupied by the Micmac Indian Chief Lone Cloud.

Accommodations: 35 rooms with private bath. *Driving Instructions:* The lodge is 106 miles east of Halifax along Route 7, the Marine Drive.

Lorneville

WEEKS' LODGE

Lorneville, Nova Scotia. Mailing address: R. R. 2, Amherst, Nova
Scotia B4H 3X9, Canada. Telephone: Ask Area Code 902
information operator for current listing. *Innkeepers:* Donna and
Jim Laceby. Open mid-May until fall.

Weeks' Lodge is just a few hundred yards from Baie Verte in the
Northumberland Strait between Nova Scotia and Prince Edward
Island. The original main house was built in 1888, and the ell was
added in 1974 with extensive modernization done by the former
owners, Mr. and Mrs. Norman Weeks.

When we inquired, the lodge had just been bought by Donna and
Jim Laceby, and they were busy making preparations for the 1980
season. Many things will be kept as they were when the Weekses had
the lodge. It is just off the road, and a single giant dark pine keeps
vigil out front. In the summer, hollyhocks add an old-fashioned air to
the yard just outside the bay window. A large expanse of mowed
meadow separates the house from the sea, and there is a secluded

600-foot beach where guests can swim in the relatively warm waters. The lodge maintains a small changing-house at the water's edge.

Inside the weathered, white-shingle building, the walls have been covered with knotty-pine paneling, and many rooms have new pine beams on the ceiling. The lodge is a popular local eatery, attracting local citizens and travelers as well as overnight guests. However, for a while after the inn opens in 1980, meals will be served only to overnight guests. Donna plans to offer her own brand of good home-cooking, with nightly offerings of roast beef, pork, breaded chicken, and seafood casseroles. She is best known among her friends as a baker, and she routinely produces such specialties as peasant rolls, Swiss braided bread, egg breads, and blueberry bread. There are no immediate plans to offer luncheons at the inn, except perhaps to guests who request them. A full American-style breakfast is included for guests on the Modified American Plan and is available as an option to European Plan guests. Rooms at the inn will have comfortable, old-fashioned furnishings, many gleaned from yard sales and local shops. The Lacebys are planning to gradually expand the number of activities available at the lodge. They are installing a playground for children (including, no doubt, the five of their own) and will offer sailboats for rent.

Accommodations: 5 rooms, 3 with private bath. *Driving Instructions:* From Amherst, continue east on Victoria Street 2 miles to Route 366, then go 18 miles northeast to Lorneville and the inn.

Lunenburg

BOSCAWEN MANOR

P.O. Box 327, Lunenburg, Nova Scotia BOJ 2CO, Canada. 902-634-8149. *Innkeeper:* Paul Chapman. Open March 1 through November.

Boscawen Manor is an old Victorian mansion built in the mid-nineteenth century. It was, and still is, the largest of the many fine homes that dot this seaside village and is considered one of the showplaces of the Maritimes. The inn is furnished throughout with Victoriana and antiques, many quite valuable. The dining room is set up with outstanding silver and crystal. The innkeeper, Paul Chapman, takes great pride in his inn and is careful to preserve its traditions, a fact appreciated by the many guests who return again and again. The rooms often have bunches of fresh and dried flower arrangements, and fires burn in the hearths on chilly or rainy days. A winding staircase, lit by the stained-glass window on the landing, is the focal point of the entrance hall. For guests' relaxation there is a den on the ground floor where the one television set resides for, in Paul's words, "those who must interrupt the quiet life." A few guest rooms have working fireplaces; all have period decor. Some rooms overlook the harbor, as do the windows in the dining room and cocktail lounge.

Mealtimes at Boscawen Manor are very pleasant and hospitable; guests relax and many fast friendships are formed over Paul's fresh local seafood dinners. The menu is explained at the table, and all meals are prix fixe. The emphasis is naturally on such "fresh from the sea" morsels as scallops, lobster, salmon, mackerel, halibut, and haddock, but there is also smoked salmon. For those "meat or die" eaters there is often a veal or Canadian ham dish. All of this is topped off by freshly made desserts. Breakfasts, lunches, and dinners are available to the public as well as to guests.

Lunenburg, with its shipyards, wharves, and many craft and antique shops, is considered a center for antique dealing and the craft capital of Nova Scotia. The town was founded in 1753 and settled by a group of Germans and Swiss. Based on the fishing and ship-building trades, it has flourished from its beginnings. The famed schooner *Bluenose* and its replica were built here, as was the replica of the *Bounty* for the Marlon Brando movie. The town's architecture is unique in Nova Scotia, and the area is very tidy, a perfect spot in which to putter about and explore. The Manor is a good place to come home to in the evenings after long jaunts around the island.

Accommodations: 16 rooms, 12 with private bath. *Pets:* Not permitted. *Driving Instructions:* Boscawen Manor is in the center of Lunenburg.

Musquodoboit Harbour

CAMELOT

Route 7, Musquodoboit Harbour, Nova Scotia. Mailing address: P.O. Box 31, Musquodoboit Harbour, Nova Scotia B0J 2L0, Canada. 902-889-2198. *Innkeeper:* P. M. "Charlie" Holgate. Open all year.

Camelot is where Charlie Holgate lives, and its very lack of outward commercial appearance makes guests feel right at home. In the end, however, it is Charlie herself who welcomes all the guests and lets them relax at her home at the bend in the river. One can sit in the living room, the dining room, or several of the bedrooms and watch the river flowing over the rocks just behind a large maple tree that bursts into a red and yellow flame every fall. The twin-bedded guest rooms upstairs (and one larger room for families) are furnished comfortably, though guests tend to spend little time there, except to sleep. The focus of the inn is Charlie's dining room and living room.

Days start with what Charlie likes to call her "no lunch" breakfast. Guests gather at her large mahogany dining table and start the day with juice or fruit, whole-grain Red River cereal (stone-ground wheat and rye laced with whole flax and cooked with raisins), a choice of bacon, sausage, or ham, and two eggs any style. Her eggs come from local free-range hens and their flavor is never found in the city; and her breads are made from whole stone-ground flours. Her jams include blueberry (a favorite with guests), strawberry, peach marmalade, plum, and others made from the fruits of the moment. Breakfast plates are always garnished with fresh lettuce, tomato, and parsley—Charlie is known to friends and guests as "the parsley freak."

Lunch is not served at Camelot, and dinner is often timed as much to suit the schedule of guests as Charlie's. Dinners here usually follow the same pattern and are served, with twenty-four hours' notice, to houseguests only. After a cocktail hour (beer, sherry, or juice) in the living room, the dinner starts with one of Charlie's homemade soups (cream of spinach and cream of asparagus are two favorites) and continues with the salad of the day, usually a combination of greens and vegetables and often fresh from her garden. The dinner entree (fresh fish, curry, coq au vin, coquilles Saint Jacques, or seafood casserole) is accompanied by potato or rice and a fresh vegetable. Wine is served with dinner. Charlie was recently in a quandary over the rising price of food and wines, so this policy is still up in the air for the coming year. In any event, we can trust her to make the best decision for Camelot and its guests. After dinner, guests usually move into the living room by the fire for dessert and coffee. Favorites are blueberry, apple, cherry, or lemon pie, apple crisp with whipped cream, lemon snow, or gingerbread. Guests can influence the menu of the day, but most prefer to let Charlie operate without interference. Evenings by the fire give guests a chance to share the day's experiences and often to form permanent friendships with other guests and with Charlie herself.

Accommodations: 5 rooms sharing bath. *Driving Instructions:* The inn is on Route 7, about 30 miles east of Halifax.

RIVERSIDE

Musquodoboit Harbour, Nova Scotia BOJ 2LO, Canada. 902-889-2440. *Innkeepers:* R. J. and Mrs. Sutton. Open all year.

Riverside stands on the banks of the Musquodoboit River surrounded by 8 acres of woodland, pastures, and a large organic vegetable garden. This informal, easygoing retreat and its unique innkeepers have been attracting guests for some twenty years. Riverside began as a sportsmen's retreat for Colonel Sutton's hunting and fishing buddies. Soon the Suttons were besieged with requests from many tourists who had heard of the couple and their unspoiled inn. Riverside is very much the Suttons' private home, and guests are treated as special friends.

The lodge is a dark log building that began its life in the mid-nineteenth century as a stagecoach stop. It still retains the look and feel of the turn of the century. Rooms are simply furnished with utilitarian period antiques and comfortable overstuffed chairs and couches. Coffee and home-baked cookies are served in a living room lined with well-stocked bookshelves. The guest rooms are rather austere, much like those in the summer hotels of the early 1900s. Often filled with the hushed sounds of winds in the trees and the murmuring river, they play an important part in the nostalgic trip back in time. This atmosphere is no illusion, as every meal attests. Almost all the food is produced organically on the grounds. Colonel Sutton feels that growing your own—whether lambs, ducks, or seed-started vegetables—assures top-quality foods. At Riverside guests will find pigs, chickens, ducks, lambs, and the organic garden. Excess produce is given to local fishermen who, in return, often supply the lodge with freshly caught salmon, sea trout, or eels. Mrs. Sutton is an excellent cook, and meals feature many of her own recipes. The combination of fine home-cooking and high-quality unadulterated foods makes all the difference. Those who are not guests of the Suttons but wish to enjoy a meal here can call a day or two in advance for a reservation.

The Suttons, a warm, outgoing couple who truly enjoy people, provide guests with a friendly, entertaining stay in a rural setting far from modern cares. There are long, sandy beaches, clams waiting to be dug, and rivers filled with salmon.

Accommodations: 7 rooms with private bath. One cabin available in summer months. *Pets:* Permitted with advance planning and only if well behaved. *Driving Instructions:* The inn is reached from Halifax via Porters Lake and Route 7. There are signs on the highway. The lodge is down a country lane.

Parrsboro

OTTAWA HOUSE BY THE SEA

Parrsboro, Nova Scotia. Mailing address: P.O. Box 98, Parrsboro, Nova Scotia BOM 1SO, Canada. 902-254-3041. *Innkeepers:* Peter and Winnie McCaig. Open June 1 to October 15.

Ottawa House was built by John Ratchford, an English gentleman, in 1780. A leading citizen of the region, Ratchford was instrumental in promoting trade, commerce, and lumber. However, Sir Charles Tupper was the most famous resident of Ottowa House. He was the premier of Nova Scotia in the 1860s, a leader in the drive to form the Dominion of Canada, a member of the Canadian Parliament and a cabinet member for a number of years. He served as prime mininster for a few months in 1895 before being defeated in the next elections by Sir Wilfrid Laurier. On the opposite side of the coin, another illustrious owner of Ottawa House was Carl Merriam, a rum-running sea captain who used the building as a front to run liquor into the United States. He was arrested and found guilty, but he escaped punishment by dying the day before his sentence was pronounced.

Ottawa House has been an inn since 1924. The rustic log structure's guest rooms have ocean views. Each opens onto the veranda or second-floor balcony, where guests can sit and watch the tide rise and fall up to 55 feet every twelve and a half hours. The inn is

a good base for exploring some of the finest coastline in the Maritimes. Guests can gather dulse, driftwood, agates, and amethyst as well as swim, fish, and go clamming.

But it is the food that first draws many guests to Ottawa House. The inn has been featured in *Where to Eat in Canada* for several years and has been highlighted in articles both in Maritime newspapers and the *New York Times*, and on CBC-TV. Its reputation is based on a relatively small offering that permits using only the freshest locally available ingredients. The menu, though small, changes daily, and there are hundreds of possibilities each season. Dinner begins with a choice of appetizer—like steamed clams or lobster and escargot-stuffed mushrooms—or salad of the day. There are usually three entrees, such as breast of chicken with apricot brandy sauce, Atlantic salmon with lobster stuffing, cod cheeks and tongues, or flounder meunière with walnuts and banana chips. Desserts are also varied and often include strawberry Romanoff, peach crisp, hot blueberry pie, or a cheese-and-fruit tray. Reasonable entree prices include salad or appetizer, and beverage.

Between meals, guests might like to investigate the Parrsboro Museum, which exhibits local gems and minerals. The Springhill Miners Museum, a 30-mile drive away, is also interesting.

Accommodations: 12 rooms, 4 with private bath. *Pets:* Permitted in glassed-in veranda only. *Driving Instructions:* Take Route 2 to Parrsboro, and then ask instructions in the village.

THE WHITE HOUSE

Upper Main Street, Parrsboro, Nova Scotia. Mailing address: P.O. Box 96, Parrsboro, Nova Scotia BOM 1SO, Canada. 902-254-2387. *Innkeeper:* Mrs. Muriel McWhinnie. Open all year. The White House is true to its name: a white two-and-a-half-story building with gables jutting out in every direction. Built about a hundred years ago, it was owned by the village doctor for many years. The small, family-style inn's bright bedrooms are furnished with a mixture of old and new things. Guests may also stay in a bungalow. Both it and one guest room have fireplaces. Mrs. McWhinnie takes pride in her flowerbeds and shrubs; in the summer, she provides a group of chairs out back for lounging.

Meals at the inn vary according to what is in season and lean heavily to seafood. Halibut, flounder, clams, haddock, and scallops appear frequently. The inn serves lobster occasionally, when it is available at a reasonable price. Freshly made, steaming hot seafood chowder is an almost daily specialty as are fresh berry pies. Meals are prix fixe and include soup or juice, entree, salad, homemade breads, and dessert.

Accommodations: 5 rooms with shared bath. *Driving Instructions:* Take Route 2 into Parrsboro.

Upper Granville

HARVEST INN

Route 1, Upper Granville, Nova Scotia. Mailing address: R. R. 1, Granville Ferry, Nova Scotia B0S 1K0, Canada. 902-665-2531.
Innkeepers: Bob and Chris Powell. Open June 15 to September 30. Harvest Inn, a simple farmhouse inn offering bed, breakfast, and views of the Annapolis River, is on 85 acres of land. The sturdy white house was built near the turn of the eighteenth century and remains today much as it was then. The original tracts of land in this area were long, narrow strips that ran from the river directly back over the north mountain to the Bay of Fundy. Many of these plots were deeded to British soldiers who served at Fort Anne in the mid-eighteenth-century. The remains of old Acadian homesteads are still being discovered in the surrounding area.

The rooms in Harvest House are bright and spacious with floors refinished to the original wide-pine boards. They have a variety of old-fashioned wallpapers and are furnished with antiques. Complimentary evening tea is served in the lounge, where guests can relax or play cards. In warmer months a picnic table and lawn chairs are available on the lawn.

Accommodations: 4 rooms with shared bath. *Pets:* Not permitted. *Driving Instructions:* The inn is on Route 1, 4 miles west of Bridge-town and 8 miles east of Annapolis Royal.

THE SENATOR GUEST HOME

Sunrise Trail—Route 6, Wallace, Nova Scotia. Mailing address: P.O. Box 171, Wallace, Nova Scotia BOK 1YO, Canada. 902-257-2417. *Innkeeper:* Ethel Miller. Open May 15 through the month of October.

The Senator is a stately historic home dating from the 1840s. Little has changed here over the years. Only a veranda and sunporch have been added, to provide clearer views of Wallace Harbor. The house was originally the private home of the Honorable Senator Alexander MacFarlane, one of the "builders" of the Canada Confederation. The senator's library remains in the house today; almost a thousand leather-bound law books fill the floor-to-ceiling shelves. Here are all the records of the sessions of both houses of Canada's Parliament from 1864 to 1888.

The 2 acres surrounding the Senator are dotted with many flower gardens and large shade trees, such as birch and spruce. An old lighthouse stands at the harbor's edge just across from the house. The lighthouse area, a parklike setting, offers trailer and tent camping facilities.

The gingerbread house is finely crafted from stem to stern. The 3-foot-thick cellar walls enclose a built-in wine cellar and separate vegetable-storage room. On the first floor, 12-foot-high ceilings still retain the ornamental moldings and trim. There are five marble fireplaces in the house, two in the upstairs guest rooms. All are used often, especially in early spring and late fall. The living and dining rooms are bright and airy with many fine period antiques, love seats and ornate gilded mirrors among them. Mrs. Miller's prized possessions include two gatelegged tables, one of solid oak and the other of mahogany.

The guest rooms upstairs in the big house are sunny and spacious, furnished comfortably with period antiques. A few feature water views; two have the fireplaces mentioned above. A favorite activity of guests is exploring the many nooks and crannies. On the ground floor are two kitchens: a huge servants' kitchen, which has a stone oven that can bake twenty loaves of bread at a time; and the main kitchen, which has an unusual bricked-in stove imported from England.

Guests, lodgers, and public enjoy meals here from an extensive menu that features fresh, well-prepared seafoods, particularly lobster

dishes. Favorites include Mrs. Miller's fish chowder, fresh strawberry shortcake, and lemon cheesecake. Several varieties of casseroles include haddock, trout, chicken, and ham, and all are accompanied by fresh vegetables—new beets, carrots, or peas—and rolls or brown breads. Meals are served in the attractive Victorian dining room or out on the sunporch with its harbor views.

One unusual attraction, which appeals to many interested in the occult, is the occasional appearance of a phantom ship. According to the locals, the spectre of a flaming ship has appeared in every town and hamlet along the coast of Northumberland Strait. It is said to be the *Roving Princess*, a pirate ship doomed forever to cruise the sea in flames and torment. The ship's appearance is said to bode ill for the area, bringing wrecks, storms, and death. Phantom or no, the seascapes here are outstanding.

Accommodations: 5 rooms, 4 sharing hall baths. *Pets:* Not permitted. *Driving Instructions:* Take Route 6 (Sunrise Trail) out of Amherst for about 40 miles to Wallace. The Senator is ¼ mile east of town, across from the lighthouse.

VILLAGE INN

Village Road, Whycocomagh, Nova Scotia. Mailing address: P.O. Box 22, Whycocomagh, Nova Scotia BOE 3MO, Canada. 902-756-2002. *Innkeepers:* Alex and Donna Somerville. Open all year.

The main building of the Village Inn was constructed more than eighty-five years ago and has served as an inn for the past seventy. The inn is bordered by a white three-rail fence and a variety of trees and bushes. Jutting from its roof are a number of little dormers overlooking the porch below. Within, the Somervilles have maintained the old-fashioned country look with patterned wallpapers, gingham checks on the tables, and their collection of antique dishes on display. The sole television set is in the sitting room, where guests gather every evening. The nearby housekeeping cabins carry out the white-with-red-roof theme of the main house. They are scattered around the property, which gently slopes from lawn to meadow to the shore of the Bras d'Or Lakes, a horseshoe-shaped bay on Cape Breton Island's coastline.

Meals at the Village Inn feature a number of regional products, particularly seafood. The dinner menu offers poached halibut and salmon as well as Digby scallops, lobster, and a fisherman's platter. There are steaks and pork chops for meat lovers. Most of these items are available at lunchtime, as are a number of soups and sandwiches. In addition to the usual breakfast items, the Village Inn will prepare lobster omelets for those who like to start the day with seafood. After a hearty breakfast, guests might like to go to the nearby Micmac Indian reserve, where reservation gift shops offer a large selection of handmade baskets. A pleasant side trip is north on Route 105 to the Little Narrows ferry and across to Iona and the Highland Village Museum, a reconstructed Scottish town.

Accommodations: 13 rooms, 7 with private bath, and several housekeeping cabins. *Driving Instructions:* The inn is 30 miles from the Canso Causeway via the Trans-Canada Highway (Route 105). The Village Inn is almost a mile off the highway, on the shore of one of the Bras d'Or Lakes.

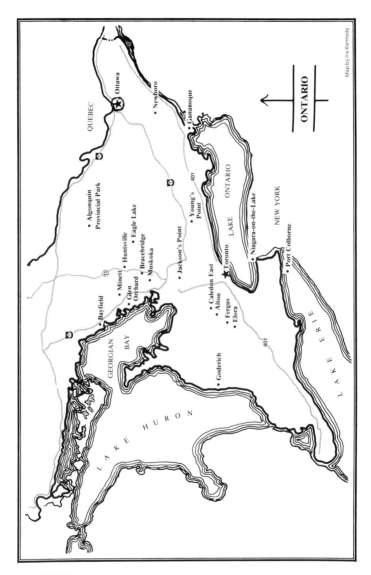

Map by Ira Kennedy

ONTARIO

QUEBEC

Ottawa

Newboro

Gananoque

Algonquin Provincial Park

401

Young's Point

LAKE ONTARIO

NEW YORK

Huntsville

Eagle Lake

Minett

Bracebridge

Muskoka

Jackson's Point

Toronto

Niagara-on-the-Lake

Port Colborne

Bayfield

Glen Orchard

Caledon East

Alton

Fergus

Elora

GEORGIAN BAY

Goderich

401

L A K E   E R I E

L A K E   H U R O N

Ontario

Algonquin Provincial Park

AROWHON PINES

Algonquin Provincial Park, Ontario. Mailing address: Huntsville P.O., Huntsville, Ontario POA 1KO; Winter: 147 Davenport Road, Toronto, Ontario M5R 1J1, Canada. 705-633-5661 (off season: 416-923-7176). *Innkeepers:* Helen and Eugene Kates. Open mid-May to mid-October.

With just under 3,000 square miles of wilderness, Algonquin Provincial Park is Ontario's largest, a land of lakes, rivers, and forests filled with wildlife ranging from myriad birds to families of moose. The bear sightings common in earlier days have been virtually nonexistent for more than a decade. Although the park has been kept an enforced wilderness by the provincial parks department and is largely accessible only by canoe, Route 60 does transverse its southern portion; only a few miles off Route 60 by private road is one of Canada's outstanding rustic resorts.

Arowhon Pines started as an offshoot of nearby Arowhon Pines Camp. Both projects were the vision of Mrs. Lilian Kates, who was drawn to the region in the 1930s. After her children's camp became successful, she sought to build a resort for visiting parents and the general public. She obtained a piece of property on the shores of Little Joe Lake and engaged architect Charles Coleman of Cleveland to design a group of log buildings that would offer first-class accommodations in a way that would intrude as little as possible into the unspoiled shoreline. The result was a group of buildings ranging from a few one-room cabins to twelve-bedroom larger cottages and dominated by a hexagonal shorefront dining room. Each overnight cabin is served by a central sitting room or lounge with a stone fireplace. Guest-room walls blend peeled logs, pine paneling, and a variety of printed wallpapers. Furnishings thoughout the resort are a blend of rare Canadian pine antiques and comfortable, more modern

furniture. Everywhere the warmth of native woods is dominant in the decor.

The dining room's hexagonal walls are made of chinked logs, and a stone fireplace rises to the center of its cathedral ceiling. Within these walls, guests are treated to the day-long appeasement of their hunger that has made the inn famous. Buffet-style dining is the rule for at least part of the meal. Guests help themselves to starters of cereals, fruits, and porridge at breakfast, then order eggs, breakfast meats, and hotcakes for table service to complete the meal. The luncheon and dinner buffets offer numerous salads and cold plates. There is a selection of hot dishes at lunch, and a more elaborate evening version might include trays of pot roast, beef en brochette, Arctic char, chicken cacciatore, stewed veal, stuffed cabbage, or lasagna. Guests are welcome to have seconds at no additional charge, and the dining rooms are also open to the public. The resort's coffee house is open most of the day and evening.

Arowhon Pines, whose name is a blend of the word "arrow" and the title of Samuel Butler's Utopian novel, *Erewhon*, is a full-fledged resort that offers many activities including swimming, canoeing, sailing, windsurfing, fishing, shuffleboard, birdwatching, and the opportunity to observe the park's wildlife. All boats, except outboard motors and windsurfers, are free to guests.

Accommodations: 50 guest rooms and suites with private bath. *Pets:* Not permitted. *Driving Instructions:* Take Route 60 into Algonquin Provincial Park. The lodge is on a private road 5 miles north of the highway; turn about 10 miles from the park's west gate.

Alton

THE MILLCROFT INN

John Street, Alton, Ontario LON 1AO, Canada. 416-791-4422 or 519-941-8111. *Innkeeper:* Christopher V. Davies. Open all year.

The Millcroft Inn is a renovated and reconstructed nineteenth-century stone knitting mill in the village of Alton and surrounded by the Caledon Hills. In 1881, the year the mill was built, Alton was an important industrial town with two woolen mills, two grist mills, a sawmill, and several factories, all drawing power from the cold, clear waters of the Credit River. A great flood in 1888 destroyed most of the mills but spared the Alton Knitting Mill to become a major producer of woolen underwear sold nationwide. Only in 1960 did pressure from competition with synthetics and a diminished demand for its product finally cause the mill to close. Recently its doors opened once again to reveal a totally reconstructed interior blending clean, contemporary lines with materials—stone, wood, and plaster—of the past.

Millcroft offers guest rooms in the old mill and in a series of townhouse-like ''croft'' houses just across the river from the mill. The houses consist of two-room units with upstairs bedrooms and downstairs sitting rooms with fireplaces. The mill's twenty-two rooms are linked by elevator to the public areas. Each room offers a different view of the millpond, the falls, the surrounding hills, or the village of Alton. They have carpeted floors, darkly stained beams that contrast with white walls, and a variety of selected antique Canadian furnishings.

Dining at Millcroft tends to be a visually satisfying experience. One can choose to eat outside under canvas at the river's edge, within the main interior dining room overlooking the pond, or in a small, glassed-in dining area that juts off the inn's stone walls, suspending diners at what seems like arm's-length from the waterfall. All meals at the inn are open to guests and the public and are chosen from à la carte menus. The many specialties are influenced by Continental schools of cuisine. Starters could be celery root with yogurt and walnuts, marinated shrimp, terrine of rabbit with cranberry and red wine sauce, or caviar Malossol. Unusual soups include consommé with gnocchi, iced avocado and chestnut, or iced yoghurt and pistachio. Recent entree offerings revealed a dozen choices including filet mignon wrapped in puff pastry, roast rack of lamb, collops of veal baked with zucchini, roast duck with cranberry and orange sauce, saddle of rabbit, fillet of Dover sole, and fresh poached salmon.

The list of things to do at the inn is extensive and in summer includes tennis, swimming in a heated pool, use of the sauna, whirlpool, and exercise rooms, and golf at a nearby course. In the winter there is cross-country skiing on the inn's 100 acres or downhill skiing on nearby slopes. The area around Alton has dozens of fine antique and craft shops. Ask at the inn for directions to the closest ones.

Accommodations: 42 rooms with private bath. *Pets:* Not permitted. *Driving Instructions:* From Toronto or London, take Route 401 to Route 10, exit north. Take Route 10 about 25 miles to Caledon village and turn left on Route 24, then go 3 miles to Route 136, turn right, and continue into Alton. Turn left at the main crossroads and drive a half mile to the inn.

Bayfield

THE LITTLE INN

Main Street, Bayfield, Ontario. Mailing address: P.O. Box 102, Bayfield, Ontario NOM 1GO, Canada. 519-565-2611. *Innkeeper: Chris Gowers. Open all year except Christmas Eve, Christmas Day and Boxing Day.*

The village of Bayfield was laid out in the early nineteenth century by Captain Wolsey Bayfield on behalf of Baron de Tuyle, a Belgian nobleman who had dreams of Bayfield becoming a successful port city. When the railroad bypassed the town, it died for a while, to revive in the 1930s as a popular Lake Huron summer resort. It is well known today for its broad, tree-lined streets, village green, and its beach and marina, the largest on the lake.

The exact date of the Little Inn's construction is not known, but by 1862 it was one of eight hotels in the town. For some time it was known as the Commercial Hotel, and for a period the brick structure had an elaborate two-story wooden veranda surrounding it. The veranda has long since succumbed to dry rot, but the exterior is still the natural buff brick. The inn is surrounded by grounds that are not extensive but are well laid out with lawns and flower beds. A stone wall delineates a narrow patio where guests may sit on iron ice cream parlor chairs at little tables and enjoy a light snack.

The inn is fully furnished in period antiques, most of them collected by the previous owner, Mrs. Ruth Wallace Brown. The Victorian parlor has a marble fireplace that is always going on cold days and provides a favorite sport in winter months for cross-country skiers back from the nearby trails. There is also a private resident's lounge so that guests may completely retire from public scrutiny if they wish. The inn's main dining room seats fifty and has print papers over chair-high wainscoting. Lunch is served daily from 12 to 2 P.M.; on Sunday, brunch is served. Evening menu selections include prime ribs and Yorkshire pudding, roast pork, lamb, and turkey, as well as fresh Lake Huron fish, curried lamb, and beef Stroganoff.

Each guest room captures the feeling of the Victorian era; the two front bed-sitting rooms have views up and down the main street (one can almost imagine a stagecoach pulling up at the inn) as well as period antiques and old beds. In one is a bird's eye maple sleigh bed; in the other, a pair of matched "his and hers" beds from the same era. All rooms in the inn have the original hard oak floors.

Chris and Kathleen Gowers pride themselves on creating the atmosphere of old-world hospitality and service of a time past. Chris certainly has the credentials to bring that to pass, with hotel experience including stints at the venerable Savoy and Grosvenor House hotels in London, England, as well as at the nearby Benmiller Inn, also known for its fine service. They will be happy to direct you to the beaches, antique and craft shops, and many activities of this popular resort area.

Accommodations: 10 rooms sharing 3 baths. *Children:* Children under 14 not encouraged as overnight guests. Families welcome in the dining room. *Driving Instructions:* Bayfield is on the eastern shore of Lake Huron, on Route 21, south of Goderich.

HOLIDAY HOUSE

17 Dominion Street, Bracebridge, Ontario. Mailing address: P.O. Box 1139, Bracebridge, Ontario POB 1CO, Canada. 705-645-2245. *Innkeepers:* Jim Niven and family. Open all year.

Holiday House, the Victorian home of Muskoka's first judge, stands on the side of a steeep mountain that drops sharply to the Muskoka River and the Bracebridge Falls far below. The inn is reached by crossing a long stone bridge over the water and high waterfalls. Off the main thoroughfare on a secluded side road that reaches a dead end above the river, the house and its motel units off to one side offer panoramic views of the river, falls, and distant hilly shore. The air is filled with the muffled roar of the falls. The main house is constructed almost entirely of stone with an old wooden turreted tower rising several stories on one end. The stonework was done in the mid-nineteenth century by English stonemasons who received 75 cents a day.

Holiday House delivers just what its intriguing exterior promises, an unspoiled, old-fashioned Victorian home. The ground-floor rooms are distinctly reminiscent of *Arsenic and Old Lace*. The high-ceilinged hallway has antique chairs and a wide, carpeted stairway. Oak archways lead to interesting public rooms. To the left is a parlor with Morris smoking chairs and round, overstuffed lounge chairs. The room has antiques of many periods, Oriental rugs, a silver chandelier and an unusual fireplace with egg-and-spool woodwork around the mantelpiece. In the dining room across the hall, an ornately carved marble-topped sideboard displays antique pink ironstone tureens. A sunny ell of the bigger room is set up with tables and offers vistas of the river and treetops. Its windows are filled with pots of African violets. A small sunroom off the dining room is decked out with large windows, Victorian-looking ferns and begonias, and an Oriental rug. It is used for larger groups and private dining. The dining room offers breakfast, lunch, and dinner to guests and the public. House specialties include roast beef and many seafood dishes. A wide selection of seafoods includes poached Coho salmon, sole poached in a light wine sauce with almonds and mushrooms, and many haddock, halibut, trout, and shrimp dishes. Downstairs at Holiday House is a popular and intimate cellar bar. A stone-walled party room nearby has a stone fireplace, piano, and lounging chairs.

The upstairs guest rooms have recently been remodeled and are decorated in eclectic fashion with plants, traditional hotel furnishings, many attractive antiques, and some modern pieces. One corner bedroom offers views of the river scenery, a comfortable bed, an attractive antique desk, and an old-fashioned bath. The best room of all contains a bedroom suite that once belonged to Ontario's first postmaster general. It has carved woods, curving glass mirrors inlaid in the oak, and a bed featuring an impressive headboard that looms over the occupants like a frozen wave.

The inn's grounds consist of a sharply steep lawn, stone walls and rock gardens, and a heated outdoor swimming pool. The town is just a short walk from here, and year-round sports abound in the area. The Bracebridge region offers scenic beauty, rugged terrain, and many recreational activities.

Accommodations: 9 inn rooms and 10 motel units, all with private bath. *Pets:* Not permitted. *Driving Instructions:* From Muskoka, take Route 4 over the bridge, turn left on Ontario Street and left again on Dominion Street.

Caledon East

THE CALEDON INN

Airport Road, Caledon East, Ontario LON 1EO, Canada. 416-584-2891. *Innkeepers:* Maureen and John Brown. Open March 1 to January 2.

We discovered the Caledon Inn one bright December day, and we have been smiling ever since. We gazed across the broad field below the inn at the pale yellow and tan fieldstone building, hoping as we drove up the driveway that it was a true inn with overnight accommodations and not just a restaurant as their sign at the road implied. The inn's hillside location means entering the first floor from what appears to be a second-story veranda, under which the basement windows look out over the fields.

Once we were inside, innkeeper John Brown confirmed our hopes and invited us to browse through the antique shop that occupies the front room of the 180-year-old inn. Old pine tables are heaped with interesting pieces and local craft items. Just beyond the shop is a small living room opening directly into a sunny tearoom. An overstuffed old couch in the sitting area faces the stone fireplace and an exposed-stone wall section from the main house. The sitting and tea rooms are in a clapboard addition from long ago. The rooms have low ceilings, some revealing their dark, heavy beams. The floors have a decided rise and fall to them, with accompanying creaking noises. The walls and antique tables and hutches of pine and maple are decorated with cranberry glass, brass and iron kettles, and pieces of horse brass. The guest rooms, up a narrow enclosed staircase, have surely not changed in many years. The low eaves and walls have antique papers and the beds look about as uneven as the floors.

Some of the world's finest old inns are in the British Isles, and the Caledon offers guests a chance to sample one of their country cousins. Both innkeepers hail from the United Kingdom—John from Wales and Maureen from London. Maureen's cooking reflects her British upbringing, with a touch of French cuisine here and there. Our introduction to her kitchen was plates of piping hot quiche accompanied by the house salad and steaming mugs of mulled cider. For those who prefer, various sandwiches and a pub lunch are also available. For dessert we couldn't resist hot raspberry pie with crumbly sweet crust and topped with vanilla ice cream. Every afternoon the Browns serve Devonshire tea with scones, homemade preserves, and pastries. For dinner the house specialty is a complete roast beef and Yorkshire pudding dinner.

The inn is on 25 acres, an area that appears larger because of the surrounding farmland. The property is fine for hiking in the summer and cross-country skiing in the winter. A stream cuts through the back of the land, and an orchard's trees are laden with apples in the fall. People often ask us what our own favorite type of country inn is. Stop by the Caledon and you will know.

Accommodations: 3 rooms, 1 with private bath. *Pets:* Not permitted. *Driving Instructions:* From Toronto, take Route 401 to the Airport Road, then drive north to the village of Caledon East. The inn is a mile north of the village on the west side.

Eagle Lake

SIR SAM'S INN

Eagle Lake P.O., Ontario KOM 1MO, Canada. 705-754-2188.
Innkeepers: Mr. and Mrs. James T. Orr. Open all year.

For years the Haliburton area (of which Eagle Lake is a part) was a noted summer resort for residents of Toronto and Buffalo. Recently, however, it has become almost as popular as a winter-resort area. A major contributor to this increased winter popularity has been the success of the Sir Sam's Ski Area, which has a double chairlift, a T-bar, and slopes with runs of up to 4,000 feet. For cross-country enthusiasts, both groomed trails and pure wilderness skiing are available.

When we first heard of Sir Sam's Inn, we assumed that it would prove to be a typical modern motel-like ski-center lodging. We couldn't have been more wrong. In fact, Sir Sam's Inn was built in 1917 as a personal country retreat for Sir Samuel Hughes, who had purchased many square miles in the greater Haliburton area at the turn of the century. Sir Sam spent several years deciding exactly where to build his home amid the clear lakes and streams and thick hardwood brush. He finally selected the shore of Eagle Lake and built a two-and-a-half story, fourteen-bedroom, exposed-beam and plaster estate home. Pillars almost as tall as a man form a base for other pillars supporting a porch roof that runs the length of the front. Inside, dark-stained trim and exposed beams blend with the stone of three fireplaces and the starkness of freshly painted white walls to create a bright interior.

Guests may choose overnight accommodations from guest rooms in the main building or in one of four connected contemporary shed-roof cedar chalets. These face the lake, and each has its own small wooden deck outside a sliding glass-door wall. The rooms in the main lodge continue the theme of exposed, dark-stained window trim and white walls and ceilings broken by strips of dark wood. The furnishings blend modern beds with white wicker and traditional hotel furniture. On the walls of some rooms are mirrors made from old, many-paned windows that have been refinished.

Diners may sit by a fire in the brick fireplace of the dining room and enjoy dinners including a choice of five entrees each day. Regular offerings include a vegetarian dish, steak, roast prime rib of beef, and a daily seafood dish. Probably the most popular of these is the inn's rainbow trout stuffed with shrimp and crab. The chef also prepares a daily special that might be chicken Kiev, Polynesian pepper steak, or barbecued beef ribs, to name a few. Several desserts prepared regularly include a flaming baked Alaska.

Summer activities at the lodge include sailing, canoeing, horseshoes, wind surfing, water skiing, and horseback riding. Tennis and golf are both available nearby, and fishing is good in Eagle Lake and neighboring lakes and streams. Guests may swim in either the lake or the pool at Sir Sam's.

Accommodations: 14 rooms, 9 with private bath. *Driving Instructions:* From Haliburton, drive 10 miles north on Route 519 to Eagle Bay.

Elora

ELORA MILL INN

77 Mill Street West, Elora, Ontario NOB 1SO, Canada. 519-846-5356. *Innkeeper:* Mr. A. W. Panchuk. Open all year.

Elora, west of Toronto, was well known by early missionaries, trappers, and explorers as well as by the Native Americans, who believed their sacred spirits lived in the walls of the rocky gorge where the Grand River thunders over the waterfalls. By the 1850s, Elora was a thriving town with mills, breweries, and furniture factories. In 1842 the Elora Mill was built; it burned and was rebuilt in 1859 of handsome granite. Elora Mill, one of Ontario's largest, stands five stories high at the edge of the rushing water and falls. Once used as a gristmill and distillery, the mill is well known today as a restaurant and inn. Its stark lines and small, many-paned windows are strongly reminiscent of a utilitarian Shaker structure. Great care was taken in the transformation from mill to inn, and attention was given to even the smallest detail in an effort to retain the lines of the building's interior and exterior. The dining room and cocktail lounge are done with the old post-and-beam construction exposing the granite walls. There are views of the gorge and waterfalls, and the roar of the rushing water fills the rooms.

The guest rooms are decorated with a blend of antiques and sturdy pine reproductions. Many of the brass and cannonball bedsteads have homemade quilts and guest-room walls and ceilings also have exposed beams and stone construction. The private bath with each room has old-fashioned brass pull-chain water closets. Many rooms have windows overlooking the cascade.

Outside the inn a bridge stretches across the gorge and falls. The Mill Street shopping area features a number of arts and crafts shops, interesting boutiques, and many antique shops. The area's history is explained in displays and exhibits in the Wellington County Museum, halfway between Elora and Fergus.

Accommodations: 16 rooms with private bath. *Pets:* Not permitted. *Driving Instructions:* From Route 401 take Route 6 north through the city of Guelph. Continue 12 miles north of Guelph to Elora.

Fergus

THE BREADALBANE INN

487 Saint Andrews Street West, Fergus, Ontario N1M 1P2, Canada. 519-843-4770. *Innkeepers:* Jean and Phil Cardinal. Open all year (dining room closed in January).

The Breadalbane Inn was the home of the Honorable Angus Fergusson, cofounder of the town of Fergus, west of Toronto. The mansion, constructed in 1860 of 2-foot-thick limestone quarried by Scottish stonemasons across the Grand River, was the scene of a tragic Victorian love story. In 1891, Miss Georgie Fergusson, granddaughter of the Honorable A. Fergusson, climbed out an upstairs window and eloped with a Dr. Black, a dentist from Elora. At the time of this escapade, Dr. Black's fiancee, the station agent's sister, was off in Toronto buying her trousseau. The couple went to Chicago, leaving behind debts of £400; Georgie herself left a good home and a brokenhearted father to mourn her rash step. And heaven knows what became of the poor lass and her new trousseau.

The inn stands at curbside behind a low iron-picket fence. Dark green ivy climbs the beige mortared stones and around the bay window that overlooks the treelined street. Trees shade windows opening onto the side lawns. Out back is a Victorian English walled garden with brick pathways, a small reflecting pool, triangular and rectangular gardens, and an abundance of flowers. The innkeepers have set up feeding stations to attract birds to this old-fashioned courtyard. A covered porch with iron lawn furniture opens onto the gardens.

The rooms and hallways inside the house have 12-foot ceilings, some with the original ornate plasterwork. Rooms and stairs are fully carpeted with contemporary rugs, and walls are papered throughout with prints of golds, yellows, and whites. The dining room is furnished in casual country reproductions, and a gray marble fireplace offers warmth on chilly evenings. Lunches and dinners are available to guests and the public. A complimentary Continental breakfast is served to overnight guests, even when the restaurant is closed in January. The large guest rooms are furnished with twin double beds, sofas, and rocking chairs.

Fergus, a predominantly Scottish town, is famed for its Highland Games Festival held annually in August. In winter cross-country skiing is available in the conservation area. The Cardinals will direct guests to the quarry where people go to swim and to Lake Bellwood, which has boating facilities.

Accommodations: 6 rooms, 4 shared baths and a sauna. *Pets:* Not permitted. *Driving Instructions:* Rake Route 6 north from Guelph 12 miles to Saint Andrew Street in Fergus. Turn left and find the inn.

ATHLONE INN

250 King Street West, Gananoque, Ontario K7G 2G6, Canada. 613-382-2440. *Innkeeper:* Gerald B. Schothuis. Open all year.

Athlone Inn, in Gananoque at the center of the Thousand Islands tourist area, is a brick Victorian townhouse with gingerbread-trimmed peaks and intricate stone and concrete work around the windows and doors. (There is a motel that contains six family units.) The Athlone was built in 1874 by a wealthy manufacturer, Charles Parmenter, for his bride, a belle from Toronto. The villa took three years to complete and remained in the Parmenter family until Mrs. Parmenter's death in 1903. In 1946 it became a rooming house; in

1966 it was bought by the present innkeeper-owner, Gerald Schothuis (pronounced "Shot-house"), who worked hard to return the old home to its original splendor. It was completely overhauled, then furnished with period Victorian antiques.

The inn has three intimate Victorian dining rooms, each with a marble fireplace. Here Mr. Schothuis works his magic as an internationally trained chef. He was born in Hengeloo in the Netherlands, graduated from a Swiss Hotel school, and was one of the organizers of a section of the International Culinary Arts Show held in 1954 in Bern. His love of cooking has taken him all over the world, and guests at the Athlone reap the benefits of his experience. The menu features French and Continental cuisines with a special regard to the French sauces, and each dinner is prepared to order. Entrees comprise seafoods and a variety of meats with imaginative sauces. Meals include a salad with the chef's special dressing and individual loaves of home-baked bread. There is a small, well-stocked bar for before-and after-dinner drinks.

The inn also offers seven Victorian guest rooms set off by marble fireplaces that are now merely ornamental for reasons of safety. The rooms in the inn combine a European flair with a Victorian ambience. The motel units are modern and have air-conditioning. The grounds of the inn show Mr. Schothuis's European touch; flowers are everywhere. Large tubs and flowerboxes at the entranceways overflow with blooms in season.

The town of Gananoque is the boarding point for numerous tours through the Thousand Islands by boat and plane. An old Victorian hall at the bridge on King Street contains the Gananoque Historic Museum with a large collection of military exhibits. In Half Moon Bay, an unusual non-denominational church consists of an open-air stone pulpit looking out over the water. Services are conducted with the congregation in boats on Sundays in the summer months, and everyone is welcome.

Accommodations: 13 rooms with private bath, 7 rooms in the inn, six in the motel. *Driving Instructions:* The inn is on Route 2—the Old Highway 2. It is off the 1000 Islands Parkway at Interchange 106; take Stone Street south to King Street. From Interchange 107 off the parkway take King Street southwest to the inn.

Glen Orchard

SHERWOOD INN

Off Route 169, Glen Orchard, Ontario. Mailing address: P.O. Box 400, Port Carling, Ontario POB IJO, Canada. 705-765-3131. *Innkeepers:* John and Eva Heineck. Open all year.

Ontario's Muskoka Lakes region is a vacationland of deep pine forests, rugged hills, and large, clear lakes. The terrain is hilly with strange, tortured rock formations. The Sherwood, one of the finest of the Muskoka resorts, is just over a rise on the edge of scenic Lake Joseph. The lake and lodge are both secluded. A country lane leads down to the lodge, which is on a spur of rocky shoreline surrounded by the lake and a sandy beach on three sides. Its grounds are covered with a carpet of pine needles, and tall pines grow from hillsides and mossy rocks. The landscaping close to the lodge features flower gardens and a grass lawn for summer games. The only sounds to be heard are the birds chirping and the wind in the treetops. Several small cottages are scattered under the pines and along the shore. The main lodge, built in 1939 as a summer resort, is a sprawling white clapboard inn with dark green shutters and lanterns along the walkways. Guests enter a central paneled hall and lobby. Fanning out from this are the ground-floor guest rooms, a screened-in veranda with lake views and iron porch furniture, the wide staircase leading to the second-floor guest rooms and suites, and—the focal point of the lodge—the big lounge. This room, paneled and beamed with mellow pine woods, has comfortable upholstered couches and armchairs grouped around a stone fireplace, near the picture windows, and in its library corner. Plants abound, and the reading chairs have good lighting. It is enjoyable on cold winter evenings to sit around the fire and sip cocktails or eggnog and nibble some of the cook's tarts and cookies.

Beyond the lounge is the large dining room with its white linen tablecloths, flowers, attractive place settings, and encircling picture windows with lake views. An old-fashioned air of gentility pervades; places are set with name cards, and everyone dresses for dinner. Mornings begin with choices from a full Canadian country breakfast menu. Evening meals feature a selection of three or four entrees in a multicourse meal with everything from soup to nuts (or, in this case, little dinner mints). Entrees might include duck, lamb chops with mint sauce, steaks, or a fresh, locally caught pan-fried fish. There are several homemade soups, such as corn chowder and old-fashioned tomato; a number of appetizers include smoked salmon or herring in sour cream. Dessert specialties are fruit pies, especially the rhubarb crisp.

Guest rooms in the lodge look out over the lake or into the tree-tops. Each room is carpeted and offers old-fashioned sturdy resort furniture, such as maple bedroom sets. Several rooms have spacious sitting areas with couches and coffee tables.

The Sherwood is a full-service, year-round resort with a special personal touch that can only be found in an intimate place like this. There are many indoor and outdoor activities. The main feature is the large, peaceful lake. Sherwood maintains canoes and boats for exploring and fishing, and there are rafts and the beach for swimming. In summer one can play tennis and many lawn games. In winter there is cross-country skiing, skating, snowmobiling, and any time of the year one can hike through the woodland and along the shore.

Accommodations: 17 rooms in lodge, most with private bath, 3 suites, 9 cottages, 2 with fireplaces and several with living rooms and 2 bedrooms. *Pets:* Not permitted. *Driving Instructions:* From Toronto, take Route 400 and Route 11 to Gravenhurst. From there, go on Route 169 to Glen Orchard. The inn is well signposted along the road.

Goderich

BENMILLER INN
 Benmiller, R.R. 4, Goderich, Ontario N7A 3Y1, Canada. 519-524-2191. *Innkeeper:* Robert Grant. Open all year.

Benmiller Inn near Goderich, a town on the shores of Lake Huron, seems an almost perfect marriage of historic buildings with a bold, visionary use of contemporary rebuilding techniques. At the core of this project in restoration and innkeeping are three buildings. The Benmiller Woolen Mill, a 2½-story cast-lime building, produced woolen blankets for more than a century. The Pfimmer Brothers flour- and gristmill and the adjacent mill-owner's home complete the group that formed the basis for Benmiller Inn.

 The restoration project respected the purpose of the mills and the items they contained. Instead of gutting the buildings and fabricating "motel within old walls" interiors, the new owners engaged a group of creative architects, designers, and craftsmen to take the mills' machinery and paraphernalia and use them whole or in pieces as architectural components in creating new interior spaces. Thus, most of the metal wall and ceiling light fixtures in the Woolen mill are fabricated from parts of the weaving machinery and from belt-driving pulleys used in both mills. A modern wall clock in the reception area was actually made from the wheel of a carding machine and the programming tape of an 1875 broadloom. Old machinery pieces have been made into lamps, mirrors, wall hangings, and coffee tables. Where old wood or parts that the mills could not supply were needed, the architects then turned to recently demolished historic buildings and churches in London or Toronto. Fortunately, almost all of the original water-powered turbine systems in the mills were found to be intact. At present, most of the electricity to heat and power the River Mill guest rooms and the swimming pool is produced by a pair of 1910 Barber turbines. This intact turn-of-the-century water-power system gives visitors a chance to see, in effect, a living museum of early power production.

The inn's buildings contain a variety of lounges and meeting rooms with weathered woods on the walls, exposed beams, and comfortable chairs and sofas. Because the mills' water system still functions, the lulling sound of gently rushing water can be heard in many parts of the inn. The dining room offers all meals to guests and all but breakfast to the public, by reservation. The à la carte dinner menu's starters range from prosciutto and melon to smoked salmon or chef's pâté to lobster bisque or French onion soup. Evening entrees include salmon, trout, jumbo shrimp, calves' liver, sirloin steak, and roast rack of lamb. Desserts are offered from a trolley. There is a luncheon menu most days, with a buffet on Sunday. In summer the noon buffet is offered daily.

Accommodations at Benmiller Inn run from simpler, twin-bedded rooms in the mills to suites—in the new wings added to the original mill-owner's home—that have electric fires, whirlpool baths, saunas, and separate, full-size living rooms. Four rooms in the mill-owner's house were restored to their original state and contain the original tin ceilings as well as other period architectural details.

Accommodations: 42 rooms and suites with private bath. *Driving Instructions:* The inn is 2 miles off Route 8, 2 miles east of Goderich and 8 miles north of Clinton, near Lake Huron.

GRANDVIEW FARM

Route 60, Huntsville, Ontario. Mailing address: P.O. Box 1089, Huntsville, Ontario POA 1KO, Canada. 705-789-7462. *Innkeepers:* The Craik family. Open first long weekend in May through just after Canadian Thanksgiving (in October), and December 26 to end of March.

Grandview Farm is aptly named. You pull off Route 60 just past a small barn and travel down a long drive that dips down into a vale and up onto the bluff that overlooks Fairy Lake. When we were there, skaters could be seen gliding down the lake for miles, a sight that Bruce Craik admitted was somewhat unusual but certainly grand. "Usually," he pointed out, "the lake is covered with snow at this time of the year." Although snow was surprisingly absent that January afternoon, the inn was full to capacity, and guests of all ages were having a fine time.

Grandview Farm was settled in 1874 by the Cookson family, who opened the farmhouse doors as an inn thirty-seven years later and operated it until 1968. When the Craiks bought the farm they decided to close down its operation as a producing farm and to concentrate on innkeeping. They spent more than a year renovating the farmhouse, which involved a virtual reconstruction of the entire building. The result is a gracious country home filled with family antiques in a building combining many modern amenities with architectural elements of the earlier home. The inn's entrance sets the tone of the rooms that follow; a pair of antique intertwining brass candlesticks are on a dark, carved-oak chest that could be several centuries old. The hall has an old butter churn and an ostrich that once saw service on a merry-go-round. To the left is the comfortable living room with its shelves of books, fireplace, comfortable furniture, and picture windows overlooking the lake. The dining room across the hall has antique side tables and china cabinets displaying pieces of family silver and china. When we arrived, a caldron of hot pea soup was ready to warm guests coming in from the January chill. Dinners here change daily depending on the season, but frequent favorites include poached salmon, curried lamb, chicken and dumplings, pork chops, and, on most Saturday evenings, roast beef. In summer, guests frequently dine outdoors on the screened, canvas-roofed patio.

Probably the most special of the guest rooms upstairs at the inn is the Four-poster. It has, in addition to the canopied bed for which it is named, its own four-piece bath with dressing room and a large private deck. The Daisy Room has a brass-trimmed iron bed, pink loveseat, pink rug, and green spread. Huge windows overlook the length of the lake. In addition to these innlike rooms in the main building, there are six cottages dotting the terraced hillside. Owl's Nest, for example, is a little pine cottage that sits on a stone foundation. There is also a nine-room modern building set into the hillside. Known as Tree Tops, it offers large guest rooms with sliding glass doors opening onto individual balconies. Four of these have fireplaces and refrigerators.

Grandview Farm has many activities of a resort, although the Craiks rightly feel the word does not properly convey the country-inn spirit of the place. There is tennis, golf, swimming on the lake's sandy beach, water skiing, sailing, and boating in the summer. Winter brings cross-country skiing, snowmobiling, sleigh rides, snow-shoeing, tobogganing, skating, and downhill skiing at nearby Hidden Valley and Echo Ridge.

Accommodations: 14 rooms and 6 cottages, all with private bath. *Pets:* Not permitted. *Driving Instructions:* Take Route 400 north from Toronto to Route 11 north to Huntsville. Outside Huntsville, take Route 60 east 4 miles to the farm.

Jackson's Point

THE BRIARS RESORT

Hedge Road, Jackson's Point, Ontario. Mailing address: P.O. Box 100, Jackson's Point, Ontario LOE 1LO, Canada. 416-722-3271. *Innkeepers:* John and Barbara Sibbald. Open all year.

The Briars Resort at Jackson's Point, north of Toronto, is an old family estate consisting of the Sibbald House and the Country Club, which are separated by an eighteen-hole golf course in the middle. The Sibbald House is the most innlike; other accommodations range from one-to-ten-room summer housekeeping cottages to motel-like accommodations near the original estate house. Sibbald House was built in 1838 and bought by John Sibbald's uncle from the Crown grantees about a hundred years ago. Dr. Frank Sibbald, recently returned from a medical practice in China, wanted to create a private retirement estate suitable to a man of his position. The octagonal brick house he built for his peacocks is still intact on the inn's property. When the current housekeeper's father, J. D. Sibbald, inherited the estate, he attempted to run it as a dairy farm but soon realized that the economics of doing so were not in his favor. In 1922 he converted some of the farm's pastureland into a golf course designed by the famous golf architect Stanley Thompson. The course was redesigned and enlarged in 1973 by the Canadian golf architect Robbie Robinson.

For a number of years the only guest accommodations were at the Country Club, but in 1977 the Sibbald Manor House was opened to the public as a restored reminder of an earlier era. Every room in the manor has been carefully restored, with many of the century-old pieces of Sibbald family furniture in use and on loan from the family to the inn. Bedrooms have authentic period wallpapers and a variety of antique beds and other furniture. One four-poster canopied bed has carved spiral posts. Attached to the main house by a brick canopy is a modern twenty-four unit guest building. Accommodations at the Country Club cottages are less formal.

The dining room at the Country Club is a summers-only operation and used mostly for breakfast, luncheons, and a weekly cookout. The main dining room at Sibbald House has a daily table d'hôte dinner with choices of soup or juice, salad or appetizer, and a selection of three or four entrees followed by dessert. A survey of a week's menus turned up starters like French onion soup au gratin, cream of broccoli soup, mulligatawny soup, and white asparagus wrapped in ham. Entrees ranged from roast duckling or veal cordon bleu to sauteed whole silver salmon, fillet of pickerel, or roast prime ribs of beef. The public is welcome to dine at Sibbald House; most menu items are available at a basic prix fixe charge.

It is difficult to describe succinctly the myriad acitivities available on this 200-acre estate. In summer, there is a choice between two heated outdoor pools and the 1,000-foot lakefront. There is tennis on three courts, a sauna, shuffleboard, badminton, volleyball, horseshoes, table tennis, and a special playground for children. All this, and championship golf too. For those preferring their leisure time to be more organized there are movies, card evenings, cookouts, theater nights, and so forth. The resort is now open for accommodations, cross-country skiing, and snowmobiling. Guests can skate near the century-old peacock house, snowshoe, go tobogganing, ice fishing, or try the Scottish sport of curling.

Accommodations: 50 year-round rooms plus a number of summer-only cottages, all with private bath. *Pets:* Permitted at Country club cottages only. *Driving Instructions:* Take Route 48 from Toronto to Sutton. Then drive 2½ miles to Jackson's Point via High Street and Dalton Road. Turn right and drive along Hedge Road to the resort.

Minett

CLEVELANDS HOUSE

Muskoka Road 7, Minett, Ontario POB 1GO, Canada. 705-765-3171. *Innkeeper:* Robert E. Cornell. Open mid-May to October.

At the turn of the century, before the development of the automobile, Cleveland's House was already a well-established summer resort. Its guests took the regular trains to the lakes region, then boarded the Muskoka Lakes steamship for a day-long journey that paused at each of the grand resort hotels to discharge passengers. Most of the old hotels have long since disappeared, the victims of disuse or fire. The few that have survived into the 1980s have either added garish condominiums or have been allowed to grow seedy with minimal upkeep. Happily, Clevelands House—though it has grown with the decades and has added lodges and bungalows—still manages to capture the flavor of another era.

Established in 1869, Clevelands House offers guest accommodations in two lodges, the main hotel, a renovated "Colonial House," a special three-bedroom cottage, and a group of about twenty-five bungalows with one or two bedrooms each. As inn-lovers we particularly like the old-fashioned waterside hotel rooms in either the main hotel, the North Lodge, or the Colonial House. Most rooms at the resort have carpeting, private bath, individual room heat, air conditioning, and room telephones. There are exceptions; if any of these amenities are particularly important to you, be sure to ask for them.

The public rooms in the various buildings now vary from the modernized, paneled look of North Lodge, with its upholstered furniture and stone fireplace, to the more old-fashioned country-inn feeling of the main lounge in the hotel. This lounge has dark-stained ceiling beams, area Oriental rugs over wall-to-wall carpeting, print wallpapers, and leather easy chairs. Rough-hewn beams, log walls, and modern lounge chairs mark the Pioneer Room, where guests gather for cocktails. The hotel's main dining room features linen table service; men are still asked to don jackets for the evening meal, and ladies should wear pants suits or dresses. Because Clevelands House is an American Plan resort, menus change daily but generally follow the same pattern. Dinners start with a choice of soup or juice followed by salad. There are usually five entrees with such selections as roast beef with Yorkshire pudding, sautéed medallion of pork, grilled salmon, seafood salad, beef Stroganoff, or bacon omelet. Entrees come with vegetables of the day and are followed by a choice of about four daily desserts. Luncheons feature somewhat lighter offerings but have a wide variety of choices and several courses.

Clevelands is a major sports resort with tennis on sixteen well-maintained courts leading the list of activities. It is the home of the Muskoka Lakes Tennis Championships and special five-day tennis clinics. Its location on Lake Rosseau means that many of its resort activities center on the waterfront. In addition to swimming and boating, the resort offers instruction at its water-skiing school. There is good fishing for lake trout, bass, and pickerel for which guests should obtain a license. Clevelands plans to open its Maple Hills nine-hole golf course this year with nominal daily greens fees for guests. Riding is not offered at Clevelands, but there are two riding stables about 15 miles away.

Accommodations: 150 rooms, most with private bath. *Pets:* Not permitted. *Driving Instructions:* From the south, take Route 400 from Toronto to Barrie, then Route 11 to Bracebridge. In Bracebridge, take Route 118 west through Port Carling to Muskoka Road 7, then take a right to the hotel.

Muskoka

WINDERMERE HOUSE

Windermere, Muskoka, Ontario P0B 1P0, Canada. 705-769-3611. *Innkeeper:* Miss M. E. Aitkin. Open June 1 through late September.

Overlooking Lake Rousseau, surrounded by well-kept grounds of sloping lawns, flower gardens, and meadows, is historic Windermere House, one of Ontario's early resorts. This old-fashioned, full-service summer place is in the best of resort traditions, offering every activity and service a vacationer could ask for. The white-clapboard main house with its red roof has two towers flanking the second-floor veranda that stretches across its façade. It has candy-striped red and white awnings, and flags flutter from the tower peaks.

In 1862 a young Scot from the Shetland Isles, Thomas Aitkin, came to the wilderness frontier of Muskoka and landed his dugout canoe on the sandy beach at the site where the big hotel now stands. Soon after, he built cabins to accommodate the travelers and sportsmen coming to the newly opened-up area. From that pioneering start

Aitkin developed the Windermere House, which has grown over the years in keeping with modern improvements but has remained in the same family. Aitkin began the main building in 1870 and added to it in 1883 and again in 1903. It was built along the lines of the Victorian resorts of the day with large, bright, high-ceilinged rooms that have French doors and windows. The main lounge, with an impressive stone fireplace and comfortable groupings of overstuffed couches and chairs, is a favorite gathering place for guests who enjoy chatting.

In 1972 and 1975 two new sections containing luxury suites were constructed near the lodge; Terrace and Settler's Bay. Both are quite modern with terraces and glass sliding doors overlooking the lake and the flowers in beds and along landscaped paths.

The main building has recently been extensively updated and modernized. There are a number of specialty shops on the lower level. Among the indoor facilities are the Sun Room, a reading and letter-writing area; the Libary; the Pioneer Room with such games and recreations as table tennis and nightly informal get-togethers and dances. On Sunday nights full-length movies are shown in this room. Full-course dinners, lunches, and breakfasts are served in the main dining room; snacks and refreshments are available in the downstairs parlor and on the patio; and the Birdcage Room offers cocktails.

A variety of accommodations are offered including simple and inexpensive yet comfortable rooms and family suites that share baths; larger rooms with private baths; and luxury sitting room–bedroom suites and second-floor veranda suites with private decks overlooking the lake. All rooms have views of either the lake of the gardens and are on all three floors of the hotel. Each suite in the nearby modern units has a living room with fireplace and cocktail refrigerator, a deck, bathroom–dressing area, and maid service.

The lake provides much of the resort's outdoor recreation and scenery. There is boating, water skiing, sailing, water polo, swimming, sunbathing on the sandy beach, and lake cruises in the launch *Viola*. Cruises take guests around Lakes Rousseau, Joseph, and Muskoka; on popular moonlight cruises; and on shopping jaunts to Port Carling. A large heated swimming pool is nearby, and across the street is the hotel's championship eighteen-hole golf course. Its grounds have an archery range, tennis courts, shuffleboard, and more—something for every member of the family.

Accommodations: 90 rooms, 65 with private bath. *Pets:* Not permitted. *Driving Instructions:* From Bracebridge, Ontario, go 19 miles northwest to the western terminus of Muskoka Road 4 and the inn.

Newboro

STIRLING INN

Newboro, Ontario KOG 1PO, Canada. Winter mailing address: General Delivery, Sydenham, Ontario, Canada. 613-272-2435 (season); 613-376-3749 (winter). *Innkeepers:* Dudley and Audrey Hill. Open mid-May through mid-October.

Stirling Inn, a homelike rooming hotel from the early 1830s, originally served travelers on the route between Kingston and Ottawa. It is next to the Newboro Locks on the scenic Rideau Canal System of lakes and waterways. The Newboro Locks were once known as the Isthmus; many engineers and sappers (trench diggers) lost their lives here because of "swamp fever" while building the Rideau system. In 1860 the hotel was enlarged to its present size. A wraparound veranda stretching the building's length has summer chairs and an old-fashioned floral-cushioned glider of the kind no self-respecting porch would be without in the old days. The hotel is built of decorative stone blocks painted white and accented by dark green trim and dashes of color from the tubs and windowboxes of geraniums on the porch.

The interior is inviting, with sunlight streaming through large windows that overlook the lawns, trees, and lakeside. The parlor lounge has a red carpet, green overstuffed chairs, matching drapes trimmed with white fringe, a red-painted wall, and green plants on the window sills.

In redecorating the intimate dining room the Hills have exposed the posts and beams and put up old-fashioned small-print wallpaper in one area, leaving the white plaster walls bare in the other. The innkeepers' collection of copper kettles and pans roost on the stone fireplace mantel and the cross-struts that have been left exposed. House specialties served here include roast beef with Yorkshire pudding, steak and kidney pie, grilled fresh salmon, and Wiener schnitzel with mushroom sauce. The specialty entrees vary each evening, and the meals come complete with soups, breads, fruit pies, and other baked goods fresh from the inn's kitchen.

This inn is a warm, old-world place that appeals to those seeking quiet, out-of-the-way lodgings. The Rideau Canal has walking trails along its banks, and fishing and boating are available at the hotel. The Hills can direct guests to the area's many seasonal flea markets and auctions. Lake cruises are also available nearby.

Accommodations: 24 guest rooms, 19 with private bath and the rest sharing. *Driving Instructions:* From Kingston, take Route 15 to Crosby, then Route 42 to Newboro. From the Thousand Island Bridge, take Route 32 and then Route 15N to Crosby, then Route 42 to Newboro. The inn is on the highway in the village.

THE ANGEL INN

224 Regent Street, Niagara-on-the-Lake, Ontario L0S 1J0, Canada. 416-468-3411. *Innkeeper:* T. J. LeDoux. Open all year. Don't let the Angel Inn's exterior and back-street location fool you. Step through its doors and you go back in history into surroundings that still seem to echo to the sounds of the British regulars of two centuries ago gathered here for food and drink. In fact, the Angel celebrated its anniversary in 1979. Built in 1779 as a three-room log cabin called the Harmonious Coach House, it was host to Alexander Mackenzie, the explorer who opened the Northwest Passage; Governor John Graves Simcoe; and Thomas Moore, the Irish national poet. In 1792 the Canadian Assembly passed the first Parliamentary Act for the abolishment of slavery in the world and celebrated the event over dinner at the Harmonious Coach House that evening. Most of the

town was razed during the War of 1812, and the Harmonious was badly burned. However, it was rebuilt on its foundations in 1815 by Richard Howard, who is said to have renamed it the Angel after his pet name for his wife.

As you sit in any of the three dining rooms at the Angel, you are well aware that history surrounds you. Hand-hewn beams are exposed on both walls and ceiling, and the plank floors that were laid in 1815 gleam today. The dining room has heavy pine tables built by innkeeper T. J. LeDoux from 3-inch-thick slabwood set on sewing-machine-table bases. Surrounding these are turned-pine chairs. The Angel's fine meals include unusual starters like crab-stuffed mushroom caps with cheese sauce, shrimps d'amour, and California hot peppers with béarnaise sauce. The nine regular main offerings include such diverse selections as braised beef in wine sauce, schnitzel Vienna style, duckling à l'orange, veal Oscar, stuffed sole, and a New York cut of steak with onion rings and béarnaise sauce.

The guest rooms are as steeped in history as the public rooms. Although modern bathrooms have been added, the rooms retain their early feeling with four-poster and canopied beds. One is an Irish fertility bed with an ebony canopy. The beds have antique quilts or spreads, and the companion pieces of furniture and lamps are all from earlier periods. Although there is an inn ghost (Captain Colin Swayze of the British forces, who was tortured to death during the War of 1812), it is unlikely that your restful night's sleep will be disturbed.

Even if you can't spend a night, it is worth visiting the Angel to explore the many nooks and crannies of the public rooms, which are filled with artifacts from the last two centuries collected and displayed by Mr. LeDoux.

Accommodations: 12 rooms with private bath. *Pets:* Not permitted. *Driving Instructions:* Take the Queen Elizabeth Way to Saint Catharines and exit onto Route 55, which leads to Niagara-on-the-Lake. The town's main street is Queen and the Angel is a block off Queen (watch for the sign on Queen Street), on Regent Street.

THE GATE HOUSE

142 Queen Street, Niagara-on-the-Lake, Ontario. Mailing address: P.O. Box 1364, Niagara-on-the-Lake, Ontario L0S 1J0, Canada. 416-468-2205. *Innkeeper:* Helen Greves. Open all year.

The Gate House was recently purchased by Gary Burroughs, who has made such a success of the Oban Inn (which see) nearby. The Gate

House was closed when we visited it, but Helen Greves, its innkeeper, gave us a tour of the guest rooms, which already bear Gary's decorating mark. Helen is, like us, a former schoolteacher, and she now uses her energies to welcome guests and make sure they enjoy their stay in this pleasant village.

Although the exact date of the Gate House's construction is uncertain, it was known as Wilson's Hotel in the late eighteenth century, and the first meeting of the Law Society of Upper Canada was held here in 1797. The stone building with its shingle second floor is on a corner lot surrounded by tall trees and flagstone walks. A large glassed-in front porch may be included in a restaurant operation that is currently in the planning stages. Because Gary wants to keep the quality of the Oban Inn's dining room at the highest level, he hopes to devote his full attention there. He plans to lease the Gate House's restaurant space to an independent restaurateur who will operate it according to Gary's high standards.

The overnight part of the Gate House is entered from its side entrance into a small reception area with its own fireplace. The guest rooms upstairs are warm and inviting, with floral-print wallpapers mostly in tones of blue or rose. Furnishings in the rooms blend period Victorian and traditional furniture. There are plants in each room, a mark of both Gary and Helen (although Helen will admit to a secret loathing of ferns). Complementing both the plants and the wallpapers are the antique floral drapes on the inn's windows.

Accommodations: 9 rooms with private bath. *Driving Instructions:* Take the Queen Elizabeth Way to Saint Catharine's and exit onto Route 55, which leads to the town. The inn is on Queen Street, the main street through Niagara-on-the-Lake.

THE OBAN INN

160 Front Street, Niagara-on-the-Lake, Ontario. Mailing address: P.O. Box 94, Niagara-on-the-Lake, Ontario L0S 1J0, Canada. 416-468-2165. *Innkeeper:* Gary Burroughs. Open all year.

At the corner of Gate and Front Streets, by the mouth of the Niagara River, is a three-story, mansard-roofed English country inn. The Oban, built in 1824 as the home of Duncan Malloy, a lake captain from Oban, Scotland, has been an inn for much of its history. The building also served as the officers' mess in 1914 while troops were quartered nearby.

The Oban has made a major commitment to the proper feeding of the town's populace, which swells dramatically during the famous annual Shaw Festival. Indeed, it is unlikely that the inn's twenty-three guest rooms could ever support its six dining rooms. Three of these overlook the lake and are sunny rooms decorated in whites, yellows, and greens. Three more formal rooms include the main dining room and the Victoria Room, which is done in blue and white, has period print papers over paneled wainscoting, bent-wood chairs around tables set with white cloths, fresh flowers, and silver candlesticks, and walls hung with portraits of the British royal family. The Sitting Room dining room was once the guests' lounge and now has antique tables set with cranberry candlesticks. Guests may choose from three rooms for cocktail service. The Patio, formerly the hotel's veranda, was glassed in and hung with plants to provide year round enjoyment of the river view. Shaw's Corner, a publike setting dominated by George Bernard Shaw's portrait over the fireplace, and the Piano Bar round out the Oban's lounge facilities. Lunch and dinner are on a prix fixe basis with dinner offerings at two price levels, according to entree selected. Home-made soup, juice, salad, and dessert are included. Some of the eleven evening choices are roast prime ribs and Yorkshire pudding, stuffed pork tenderloin, salmon hollandaise, Cornish hen, grilled steak, and Dover sole. Luncheon offerings include beef Stroganoff, chicken vol-

au-vent, seafood casserole, and—our favorite—steak and kidney pie.

The bedrooms' variety of furnishings blends antique pieces like four-poster beds with more modern pieces. There are individually selected print wallpapers, coordinated window curtains, and, in some cases, fireplaces, and each is air-conditioned. Niagara-on-the-Lake is an interesting town to explore at all times of the year, although it becomes crowded during the summer theater season.

Accommodations: 23 rooms with private bath. *Driving Instructions:* Take the Queen Elizabeth Way to the Route 55 North exit. Follow the signs to Niagara-on-the-Lake.

THE PILLAR AND POST INN AND RESTAURANT

King and John streets, Niagara-on-the-Lake, Ontario. Mailing address: P.O. Box 1011, Niagara-on-the-Lake, Ontario LOS 1JO, Canada. 416-468-2123. *Innkeeper:* Neil O. Foster. Open all year.

In the 1890s, when canning factories sprouted up in the area almost as fast as tomato plants, the Canadian canning industry reached its peak. Factory No. 13 soon established a reputation for its canned peaches and tomatoes brought in daily from local farms. When World War I broke out in 1914, the factory's upper floor became a supply storeroom for Polish soldiers training in Canada. Old No. 13 continued to can fruits throughout the following decades until the last can came down the line in 1957. For a period thereafter, the factory was used for the manufacture of baskets. In 1970, it was remodeled as the Pillar and Post Restaurant and shortly thereafter added guest rooms, in time to welcome Queen Elizabeth II and Prince Philip to the opening of the Shaw Festival and to a formal banquet for 230 guests.

The core of the old canning factory remains. Its sturdy, time-worn factory floors, fireplaces, exposed brick walls, and beamed ceilings supported by heavy exposed posts contribute to the decor of the guest rooms and dining areas. Furnishings throughout the inn are mainly reproductions of early Canadian pieces; many are made on the premises by Pillar and Post craftsmen, who also make items sold in the gift shop. Dinner guests are served by waiters and waitresses in costumes reminiscent of colonial times. The dinner menu features a limited number of starters, such as seafood chowder, pâté, or Caesar or spinach salad. Twelve choices for the main course range from the less expensive veal cutlet to a top-price surf and turf. In between are offerings like stuffed boneless chicken, rack of lamb, and king crab legs. Luncheons offer lighter selections, such as omelets, quiche, and crepes as well as several sandwiches.

Guest rooms have been fitted into the factory buildings. Many of these are fully carpeted and have small-print papers and coordinated drapes as well as a selection of furniture mentioned above. A third of the rooms have working fireplaces, and a number have exposed beams and handmade quilts on the beds. A few contain water beds.

Activities at the Pillar and Post include swimming in the summer in the outdoor pool and lessons in the indoor golf school. There are saunas, a whirlpool bath, and a health club, and golf is available at two nearby courses.

Accommodations: 61 rooms with private bath. *Pets:* Not permitted. *Driving Instructions:* Take the Route 55 North exit of Queen Elizabeth Way and follow the signs to the town.

PRINCE OF WALES HOTEL

6 Picton Street, Niagara-on-the-Lake, Ontario. Mailing address: P.O. Box 46, Niagara-on-the-Lake, Ontario LOS 1JO, Canada. 416-468-3246. *Innkeepers:* Henry Wiens, John Wiens, and Jim Fitzpatrick. Open all year.

The Prince of Wales Hotel began life in 1864 as a sixteen-room inn serving the lake trade that thrived even then. Named the Prince of Wales in honor of a royal visit in 1901, the hotel has had two additions in the past half-dozen years. These are so skillfully done and so visually compatible with the original building that few guests realize their more recent genealogy.

The hotel was built of red and yellow brick, and its interior walls are paneled with mahogany or covered with brown suede wallpaper. The Victorian influence is clear in its mansard roof, stylized dormers and windows, and in many of its furnishings. The dining room's adjoining heated greenhouse is used for year-round dining. The small lounge is also used as an eating area and has a working fireplace. The Continental specialties of the kitchen are rack of lamb, poached

salmon, and pepper steak at the dinner meal, and quiche and avocado stuffed with crabmeat Hollandaise at lunch. Dancing is available in "Vikki's." Guest rooms in a variety of styles include brass beds and old-fashioned four-posters. Two bedrooms have fireplaces; the Prince of Wales Room has the furniture used during his visit at the turn of the century. One luxury suite has its own kitchen and a rooftop private patio with gas barbecue. All rooms have air-conditioning, color television, and large bathrooms.

The Prince of Wale's many recreational facilities include a full-size indoor heated swimming pool, a whirlpool bath, saunas, sunrooms, an "executive" exercise room, and rooftop platform tennis.

Accommodations: 58 rooms with private bath. *Driving Instructions:* Take Queen Elizabeth Way and exit at Route 55 North. Follow the signs to the town.

Ottawa

CHÂTEAU LAURIER HOTEL

Major's Hill Park, Ottawa, ON K1N 8S7, Canada. 613-232-6411.
Innkeeper: Canadian National Hotels. Open all year.

When the Château Laurier opened in 1912 it was considered one of the finest hotels in the province. Little has changed in the ensuing three-quarters of a century to alter the Château's reigning position. Constructed of granite and light buff Indiana sandstone, the Château was built in the style of a French castle with turrets bearing mellowed copper roofing. Named after Sir Wilfrid Laurier, the eighth prime minister of Canada, the hotel offers 500 rooms and suites and banquet facilities that routinely provide state dinners for the many heads of government who come to the nation's capital every year.

Just a short stroll from the Parliament buildings, the Château has two major restaurants—the Canadian Grill and L'Auberge. Both reflect the hotel's strong association with the French culture that is so much a part of this bilingual country. The Canadian Grill offers prix fixe dinners in a supper-club setting. The dinners are usually limited to two entrees chosen from the likes of poached turbot, lobster au gratin, sweetbreads Beaumont, veal cutlet, creamed seafood, or a mixed grill. The dinners are complete, with appetizer, soup, entree, salad, and dessert. L'Auberge has an extensive à la carte dinner menu that offers several pages of appetizers, soups, and entrees.

Accommodations: 500 rooms and suites, all with private bath.
Driving Instructions: The hotel is in the center of the city, next to the Parliament buildings.

Port Colborne

RATHFON INN

Lake Shore Road, Port Colborne, Ontario L3K 5V7, Canada.
416-834-3908. *Innkeeper:* Edward Zielski. Open all year.

The Rathfon Inn, on a sweep of lawn jutting out into Lake Erie, is
surrounded by meticulously maintained lawns, flower gardens,
ornamental shrubs and bushes, and shade trees. Completely encircling the grounds is a high, 4-foot-thick wall of limestone. The inn is
constructed of the same stone, with walls about 2 feet thick. Rathfon
was built as a private home in 1794 and became an inn in 1941. The
house and an attractive converted stone barn are connected now by a
long cement-and-stone addition containing the dining room and en-

trance hall. The Rathfon had to have a fire-escape added, which detracts slightly from the lines, a fact bemoaned most vigorously by Mrs. Zielski, one of its innkeepers.

As guests enter through large wrought-iron gates in the wall, they are greeted by a long stretch of drive lined on either side with flowering crab-apple trees and seasonal flowerbeds with tulips in spring and such colorful blooms as petunias in hotter months. Acres of lawn completely encircle the inn. Out by the water, high above the shore, is a big stone terrace where guests relax and sip cocktails.

The Rathfon is very like a small resort hotel of the late 1930s and early 1940s: somewhat austere but very peaceful. The dining room, with its long row of picture windows looking out to the gardens and lake, is decorated with pale yellows and sea greens or aquas. The tables have fresh flowers and white linen. Soft golds, yellows, and aquas are used throughout the inn. The sitting room, in the old section, has a nice fireplace and comfortable upholstered couches and chairs. The inn's only television set is in this room. Coffee tables and bookshelves are stocked with plenty of reading material and guidebook information for guests.

The spacious second-floor guest rooms are furnished with colonial-style maple pieces. The lakeside rooms catch the sounds of waves on rough and windy days. The smaller third-floor rooms are particularly inviting, and many have double beds instead of twins.

The restaurant at Rathfon offers lunch and dinner to guests and the public and breakfasts only to guests of the inn. The dinner menu offers traditional fare, such as steaks, chicken, duck, roast beef, lobster tails, and lamb. All meals are accompanied by an array of freshly baked rolls, salads, appetizers, homemade soups, and several fresh vegetables. Dessert is often a special ice cream concoction or pies and cakes. Meals at the Rathfon are reasonably priced and generous.

Accommodations: 16 rooms with private bath. *Pets:* Not permitted. *Driving Instructions:* The inn is 4 miles west of Port Colbourne on Lake Shore Road. Its sign is posted at the gate of its big stone wall.

THE WINDSOR ARMS HOTEL

22 Saint Thomas Street, Toronto, Ontario M5S 2B9, Canada. 416-979-2341. *Innkeeper:* E. C. Forrester. Open all year.

The Windsor Arms, the cosmopolitan cousin to the rural Millcroft Inn, has the presence of a fine townhouse with overtones of English Tudor. The hotel is small by big-city standards, its four-story, ivy-covered brick building set on a narrow side street just a few steps away from fashionable Bloor Street and the chic Yorkville district. Once through the heavy oak doors, guests find themselves in a tall room of cream-colored stucco and exposed dark beams. Plump, leathery couches and dark antique writing desks create an Old-World atmosphere. Just off the lobby is a living room decorated with antique sofas and small chairs accompanied by assorted antiques and reproductions of English pieces.

A shiny brass elevator carries guests to the large bedrooms. The long halls and high-ceilinged rooms are decorated with wallpapers, carpets, and some fine antiques. Each bedroom is air-conditioned and has color television and private bath with old-fashioned deep tubs and heated tiles. Some larger suites have dining rooms and even kitchens. Full room-service includes meals from the hotel's much acclaimed restaurants. The Windsor Arms is also conveniently near several of Toronto's other fine restaurants.

Three Small Rooms is the collective name for the dining spaces carved out of the hotel's basement; The Restaurant, Wine Cellar, and The Grill offer meals in attractive, intimate settings. The Courtyard Café is an interesting treatment of space. A large greenhouse structure, its beams, struts, and heating ducts are all boldly exposed. The room is laid out in levels around a chef's island where dessert and salads are prepared and displayed. The menu offers a wide range of Continental cuisine, emphasizing French and Italian dishes. Dinner might begin with quenelles of pike in the crayfish-based Nantua sauce, smoked Canadian salmon, or trout with celery root salad. A soup of fresh mushrooms or iced cucumbers and pine nuts might follow. Unusual and varied entrees include serveral terrines, a galantine of capon, and pâtés along with selections of hot or cold fresh and smoked seafoods in sauces. About fourteen meat and poultry dishes include steaks, veal, lamb, and sweetbreads. An

extensive dessert menu is presented separately; if you can budge, stroll past the dessert table to size up the situation. The hotel owns two other fine eating places, Noodles and Bay Streetcar.

The Windsor Arms is ideally located, surrounded by shops, international restaurants, the Royal Museum and Parliament. Just a block or two away, the super-clean Toronto subway whisks tourists to other sightseeing attractions, such as the CN Tower; Eaton's—a shopping mall with hundreds of stores and restaurants and eighteen movie theaters under one roof; Chinatown; and the restored waterfront areas with their markets, parks, and theaters. Toronto is both a historic city and an ultramodern metropolis; the Windsor Arms is a perfect base for exploration.

Accommodations: 82 rooms with private bath. *Pets:* Check with the innkeeper. *Driving Instructions:* The hotel is on a side street (they provide complimentary overnight parking) off Bloor Street, just west of Yonge Street.

THE OLD BRIDGE INN

Young's Point, Ontario, Canada. 705-652-3661. *Innkeepers:* Harry and Mae Galan. Open all year.

The Old Bridge Inn began life as a general store in 1887. In 1895 the enlarged and remodeled brick building was reborn as a traveler's hotel. It is set among white pines, sugar maples, and oaks, woods filled with black squirrels, birds, and small golden chipmunks. The historic Trent-Severn Canal System passes by the inn at Lock 27, a parklike area surrounding the waterway. There are thirty-five locks in the canal system, which stretches more than 250 miles from the Baie de Quinte in the northeastern section off Lake Ontario to Georgian Bay off Lake Huron. A favorite relaxation at the inn is sitting on the patio and watching the parade of boats—of every shape and size—pass through the lock. The tranquilizing sound of the rushing water reaches some of the guest rooms. The inn is named for the iron bridge built in 1883 over the canal. It is now closed to traffic, but pedestrians can walk over it and watch the boats being locked through the system.

The inn's dining rooms are decorated with the innkeepers' many antiques and memorabilia. One room is paneled and features a bar and a working Franklin stove. The other room, much the same as it was in the days of the general store, has a dark oak ceiling and wainscoting. The menu specializes in barbecued ribs, steaks, and roast beef, and the favorite dessert is homemade apple pie. In summer a honky-tonk piano player entertains on Saturday nights.

In 1952 more rooms were added to the hotel. The guest rooms were updated, and contemporary hotel furnishings were installed. Four rooms still have the old washbasins.

The canal system is the area's main attraction. The locks are closed in the winter, but most towns along the waterway have information on their history and operation. Fishing is quite good in the area; the prize being walleyed pickerel. Within easy distance from the Old Bridge Inn are many recreational activities, such as boating, hiking, swimming, and, in winter, cross-country skiing.

Accommodations: 10 rooms sharing hall baths. *Pets:* Not permitted. *Driving Instructions:* The inn is 15 miles north of Peterborough, off Route 28 on South Beach Road, just before the canal.

Prince Edward Island

Brackley Beach

SHAW'S HOTEL AND COTTAGES

Brackley Beach, Prince Edward Island COA 2HO, Canada. 902-672-2022. *Innkeeper:* R. Gordon Shaw. Open mid-June to mid-September.

In the heart of the Prince Edward Island National Park seashore, Shaw's Hotel prides itself on being the oldest on the island and the oldest in eastern Canada under the same family management. Gordon Shaw's grandfather opened the hotel in 1860, and it has grown as business has. Today, it is a three-story red-mansard-roofed building with a row of dormers the length of both sides of the roof and a wraparound porch on two sides. Over the years a number of cottages have been added to the property to provide more rooms; cottage sizes range from those with single bedrooms to a large one with four bedrooms sleeping up to ten persons. Five of the cottages have either fireplaces or an open Franklin stove. The comfortable rooms offer good beds and have either private bath or hot- and cold-running water. All rooms are offered on the Modified American Plan.

The hotel's menu reflects Gordon Shaw's love of home-style cooking that uses, whenever possible, the produce and seafood that has made the island famous. A typical dinner offers choice of juice or soup, poached Atlantic salmon with egg sauce, or chicken pot pie and vegetables. Lobster makes frequent appearances on the menu. Desserts might include deep-dish rhubarb pie à la mode, raspberries and cream, and cheese and crackers. The dining room, a more recent

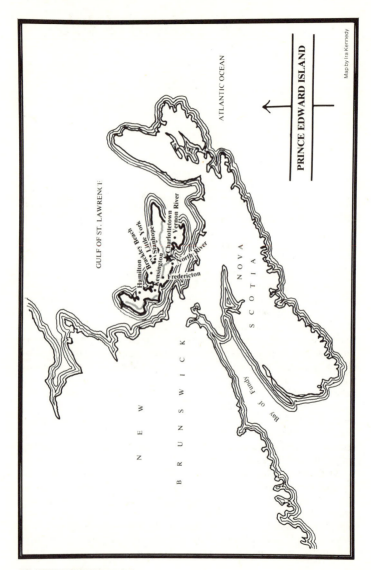

PRINCE EDWARD ISLAND

Map by Ira Kennedy

GULF OF ST. LAWRENCE

ATLANTIC OCEAN

Hamilton
Brackley Beach
Little York
Stanhope
Kensington
Charlottetown
Vernon River
North River
Fredericton

N E W

B R U N S W I C K

N O V A

S C O T I A

Bay of Fundy

addition, has a wall of windows overlooking the large lawn and the fields that stretch to Brackley Beach in the distance. Just a short walk away is swimming in 70-degree waters, which are kept as warm as those hundreds of miles to the south by the Saint Lawrence River. Sailing in Sunfish is available from the hotel, and there are also fishing, tennis, and a nearby golf course.

Accommodations: 50 rooms; of the 24 rooms in the hotel, 12 have private bath as do each of the 8 cottages. *Pets:* Permitted in the cottages only. *Driving Instructions:* From Charlottetown, take Route 15 to Brackley Beach.

Charlottetown

DUNDEE ARMS MOTEL AND INN

200 Pownal Street, Charlottetown, Prince Edward Island C1A 3W8, Canada. 902-892-2496. *Innkeepers:* Don and Mary Clinton. Open all year.

The Dundee Arms, a 1904 Victorian inn, was recently completely restored by Don and Mary Clinton to offer colonial-style dining and accommodations. When Don retired from the textile business in Montreal, he and Mary decided to retire on Prince Edward Island. The Dundee Arms Motel offered a business that was immediately available and suited to their combined business skills. After they got settled, they realized that the original Dundee Arms building would lend itself easily to restoration. As they stripped away the layers of modernization that had been added in the past seventy years, they discovered rooms with a great deal of character and charm. Today, the Griffin Dining Room has an exposed-brick fireplace, print wallpapers over blue wainscoting, and red table-linens with gingham-checked overcloths. Period-style six-armed ceiling lights provide illumination. A painting of the room's namesake hangs on one wall; cabinets against other walls display some of the Clintons' china collection.

Meals served in the Griffin and Chandler dining rooms have been touted in *Where to Dine in Canada* and in *Gourmet* magazine. Entree selections at luncheon include chicken pot pie, crepes, quiche, smoked mackerel, stuffed mushroom caps, croque monsieur, and moussaka. In the evening there are several types of fresh fish native to local waters, scallops, chicken cordon bleu, veal vin blanc, rack of

lamb, two versions of steak, and pork preville (medallions of pork sauteed, then sauced with wine, raisins, and applesauce). Guests might like to try grasshopper pie, a specialty of Mary's that consists of layers of creme de menthe–flavored whipped cream over a chocolate-wafer base.

The inn's English-style Hearth and Cricket pub combines wood and exposed brick to complement the decor of the dining rooms. The six guest rooms in the original house are where lovers of country inns should book. The remaining rooms are motel accommodations nearby. These rooms in the house are carpeted and have decorative iron and brass beds and a selection of early Canadian antiques. Rooms under the eaves have sloping ceilings.

Visitors to Charlottetown in the summer months should allow time to see at least one of the repertory performances of the Charlottetown Summer Festival. Held at the Confederation Centre of the Arts, the company puts on performances of *Anne of Green Gables* and other musicals. The Confederation Centre is open all year and includes a major art gallery, the theater, and the provincial library. Province House, the site of the birth of the Canadian nation, is today the province's legislative center. Beaconsfield, a Victorian building that houses the Heritage Foundation, has changing displays on topics relating to the island's history.

Accommodations: 38 rooms, 6 in the old inn. All have private bath. *Pets:* Not permitted. *Driving Instructions:* Take the Trans-Canada Highway to Charlottetown. Take University Avenue to Fitzroy Street, then turn right on Pownal.

SEVEN KEYS INN

Junction of Routes 2 and 227, Fredericton, Prince Edward Island. Mailing address: R.R. 4, Hunter River, Prince Edward Island COA 1NO, Canada. 902-964-2449. *Innkeepers:* Eunice Prior and Ellen Booth. Open all year. Dining room open daily in summer, Thursday to Sunday in winter.

When the Priors and the Booths approached retirement age some years ago, they developed a plan that would keep them active. Natives of Quebec Province, they decided to run a guest house on Prince Edward Island, the advantage being that they would be able to start operating the business during the summer months before they retired, then continue on an expanded schedule after retirement. The result of this careful planning was the Seven Keys Inn, named for the seven members of their combined families, and for the keys to the happiness they believed would come from their joint project. Now, nine years after they first opened the inn's doors, the Seven Keys is a continuing success, not only as a retirement project, but as a popular hostelry for travelers on Prince Edward Island. As a result of the inn's publicity in several newspapers and on television shows, many guests approaching retirement age have come to the Seven Keys for advice on starting similar establishments.

The Booths and the Priors have had fun decorating each of the guest rooms with its own authentic decor. There are the African Room, the Oriental Room, the European Room, and the Canadian Room decorated with antique Canadian pieces, a number of which belonged to the family of Prime Minister Pierre Trudeau. An antique-filled lounge is available for the use of guests.

Meals at the Seven Keys epitomize home-cooking. Mrs. Prior feels meals should be prepared according to the tastes of her guests, and she requires advance booking for all dining. At the time reservations are made, she or Mrs. Booth will discuss possible menus and then prepare a meal designed by the guests. The inn is famous for its roast beef with Yorkshire pudding and for Mrs. Prior's "secret recipe" clam chowder as well as for Mrs. Booth's array of sweets. Other frequently prepared dinner entrees include a Danish Delight of tiny spiced meatballs, beef bourguignon, fried stuffed smelts, filet mignon, scallops, spaghetti, and pork chops. Seven Keys prides itself on being a home away from home for the traveling public. On an island proud of its hospitable tradition of welcoming guests into its residents' homes, Seven Keys does the job very well.

Accommodations: 4 rooms with shared bath. *Pets:* Not permitted. *Driving Instructions:* The inn is on Route 2 at its junction with Route 227.

Hamilton

BEECH POINT VIEW FARM TOURIST HOME

Beech Point Road (Route 104), Hamilton, Prince Edward Island. Mailing address: R.R. 5, Kensington, Prince Edward Island COB 1MO, Canada. *Innkeepers:* Rowena and Alton Ramsay. Open July 1 to September 30.

Every summer Alton and Rowena Ramsey open their white shingle farmhouse to guests who appreciate its setting on an 80-acre farm and the fine views of Malpeque Bay, known for its succulent oysters. Beech Point View Farm is but one of many in this area, and the pastoral land flows gently to the nearby bay and the not too distant Gulf of Saint Lawrence. The Ramsays' home was built in 1916 on land owned by their family for a hundred years before that. Its three large double-bedded guest rooms get cooling summer breezes off the water that almost surrounds their point of land.

After breakfast, guests using the house as a vacation base are welcome to spend the day watching farm life or at the nearby beach if they are not exploring the north shore. Picnic tables and a barbecue are available to guests. The Ramsays' son Brian operates a deep-sea fishing boat, the *Fair One*, and guests frequently join him for a day's outing. Not too far away, in Burlington, are the famous scale-model castles known as the Woodleigh Replicas, which are open from mid-May to late October.

Accommodations: 3 rooms sharing bath. *Driving Instructions:* The farm is 9 miles northwest of Kensington on Route 104.

Kensington

STONE HOUSE FARM TOURIST HOME

Kensington, R.R. 6, Prince Edward Island C0B 1M0, Canada. 902-886-2651. *Innkeepers:* Rena and George Pickering. Open June 15 to September 30.

Stone House Farm was built in the mid-nineteenth century in the center of Prince Edward Island. This working dairy farm has 125 acres of rolling meadows where wildflowers bloom in season. The Pickering's sixty head of cattle, cared for by two lively Border collies, graze in a pastoral setting. A river runs along the back of the property, and a country lane leads from the main highway to the gate. Guests can enjoy the Pickerings' island hospitality in what Mrs. Pickering calls their "quiet farmhouse of distinction." Each guest room has a double bed, and guests share the washroom on the main floor. Everyone is welcome in the living room to relax, visit, have a cup of coffee, or watch television. Country breakfasts are the only meal served, but guests have the use of the fully equipped kitchen.

Lobster suppers are available daily just a few miles from the farm. These are one of the island's prime attractions and, once you have had one, you will understand why. The supper, a community project sponsored by the Lion's Club of New London, is served daily from 4 to 9 P.M. and features hot and cold lobster with melted butter, or baked ham, roast beef, or steak. Meals are accompanied by home-baked rolls, potato salad, home-made mayonnaise, cucumbers, tomatoes, and apple, lemon, or cherry pies.

Accommodations: 3 rooms sharing a bath. *Pets:* Not permitted. *Driving Instructions:* 6 miles east of Kensington on Route 6.

Little York

DALVAY BY THE SEA HOTEL AND COTTAGES

Prince Edward Island National Park, Little York, Prince Edward Island. Mailing address: P.O. Box 8, Little York, Prince Edward Island C0A 1P0, Canada. Winter: 902-892-0488; summer: 902-672-2048. *Innkeeper:* David R. Thompson. Open June to September.

Dalvay by the Sea was once the summer estate of the late Alexander MacDonald, vice-president of Standard Oil and a partner of John D. Rockefeller's. The place was named for MacDonald's birthplace in Scotland. He and his wife were world travelers who fell in love with this scenic location and commisioned the area's finest craftsmen to build an imposing mansion. No expense was to be spared. The mansion was completed in 1896, and a wing was added in 1909. Unusual cedar paneling was used throughout in varying patterns. The foyer, heated by a large sandstone fireplace, rises two stories high. The guest rooms here are off long balconies served by a wide, carpeted stairway that sweeps up from the hall below. In the MacDonalds' day the mansion was filled with antiques and art from all over the world. The stables housed the horses that pulled the family's many carriages. One carriage, a "four-in-hand," was purchased by MacDonald at a dollar a pound. The carriage weighed 1,600 pounds.

The last members of the MacDonald family to occupy Dalvay were Princess and Prince Rospigliossi, a MacDonald granddaughter and her Italian husband. Another granddaughter had married Prince Michel Murat of France. The executor of the estate lost all the extensive holdings, and almost all the furnishings were sold. Only a few pieces remain, solitary reminders of a grand and gracious past. However, the ambience is not gone; it lives on in the mansion's fine workmanship and in the beauty of the surroundings. The ocean is 200 yards from the front entranceway and a freshwater lake, landscaped with lawns and trees, extends along one side of the house. The grounds are on 15 acres of the Prince Edward Island National Park. The safe sandy beach extends for miles in both directions. The hotel provides many recreational and relaxing activities—tennis courts, a driving range, a bowling green, and canoes and boats for the lake.

Most of the inn's guest rooms are paneled with pine and have views of the lake and ocean. Apart from the old-fashioned dining room chairs of bent oak and a few older remaining antiques from the Mac-Donalds' time, the rooms are fairly austere, furnished with modern or traditional hotel-motel pieces. The splendid foyer is decked out in brightly colored vinyl chairs and couches strangely out of place in the fine room. The living room does not have many of the antiques still in place. The stone fireplace has large brass andirons and is flanked by fluted columns supporting an archway over the mantel. The ceiling is intricately panelled, and the blue walls are topped with white wainscoting. Bookcases display marble busts, and the room's rattan furnishings are attractively summery.

The hotel's dining rooms are popular with visitors to the park. They are attractively set up with fresh tablecloths and bouquets of flowers. House specialties are seafood and steaks. In addition to the lodge guest rooms there are two cottages on the grounds. The Governor General's Cottage, built for a visit by Viscount Alexander, is rented in two sections, the larger featuring a screened porch and attractive sitting room. The other cottage, small and secluded, has two bedrooms, a den, and a sitting room.

The Dalvay estate is more than just a historic mansion opening its doors to guests—it is an experience. Dalvay is immensely popular, and reservations must be made well in advance of the season.

Accommodations: 31 rooms with private bath. *Driving Instructions:* Take Route 2 east to Route 25 and the national park.

North River

OBANLEA FARM TOURIST HOME

York Point Road, North River, Prince Edward Island. Mailing
address: Cornwall, R.R. 4, North River, Prince Edward Island
COA 1HO, Canada. 902-894-8366. *Innkeepers:* John and Mildred
MacKinlay. Open all year.

The current Obanlea farmhouse, near Charlottetown on Prince
Edward Island, dates from 1884, but the history of this farming
family goes back to the late eighteenth century. Donald MacKinlay,
the great-grandfather of the present farmers, was born in Scotland in
1789. Ten years later his father died, leaving him and his brother to
support his widowed mother. After the brother emigrated to Canada,
Donald and his mother also decided to leave. They landed on Prince
Edward Island with less than ten dollars, but Donald was able to rent
a 100-acre farm in North River, where he lived for three-score years.
The MacKinlay farm has grown to more than 1,000 acres, but Donald
MacKinlay's descendants continue to farm the original land, to which
they still have the early-nineteenth-century deed.

Guests at the farm can observe an active family farm where Hereford cattle, dairy cows, a farrow-to-finish hog operation, and potato crops combine to give visitors a true picture of versatile family farming on Prince Edward Island. The farm is on the North River and surrounded with fine scenery and spacious grounds. The farmhouse has four carpeted, comfortable guest rooms. One bed-sitter sleeps four; one of the remaining three rooms can accommodate up to five people. Rooms have both modern and antique furniture, and guests share a full and a half bath. Guests have their own private entrance, and housekeeping privileges are offered. Breakfast is available for guests, and a sitting room has a color television set.

A short distance away are good local beaches, fishing, the rural lobster suppers for which the island is famous, live theater, harness racing, and more. Charlottetown, the capital of Prince Edward Island, is 4 miles away.

Accommodations: 4 rooms with shared bath. *Driving Instructions:* Take the Trans-Canada Highway (Route 1) west from Charlottetown for 4 miles, turn left onto York Point Road (Route 248), and drive to the second farm on the left.

Stanhope

STANHOPE BEACH LODGE AND MOTEL

Stanhope Beach, P.O. Box 2109, Charlottetown, Prince Edward Island C1A 7N7, Canada. 902-672-2047 (summer) and 902-892-6008 (winter). *Innkeeper:* Gerald W. Auld. Open July and August.

Stanhope Beach Lodge, on 10 acres of green peninsula jutting out into the bay, has been welcoming guests for more than a century. It stands on cliffs overlooking Covehead Bay Shore, and the property is right next to a national park with its 20-mile stretch of dunes and beaches. On a rise behind the hotel are two range lights that when aligned with a third light in the mouth of the harbor, serve to guide boats into safe waters. In their early days these lights were fueled by kerosene.

Gerald Auld, the innkeeper, is the great-great-grandson of Angus McMillan, who operated the hotel as a summer resort called Point Pleasant Hotel in 1855. Underneath the additions, wings, and porches of today's lodge beats the heart of the original McMillan cabin, which

is the small receiving room to the right of the entrance. Angus just built right over it to create a house within a house. The three dormers over the main entrance are also part of the original family home. The present hotel is a big place with seventeen motel units in addition to the guest rooms in the main lodge.

The lodge still has its turn-of-the-century antique furnishings and decor with large murals in the halls and Victorian armchairs, bureaus and commodes in most rooms. The sitting rooms and dining rooms have fireplaces and views of the sea and lawns. A prime dining attraction in the area is the hot and cold lobster smorgasbord served in the North Shore dining room and featuring a spread where guests can have their fill under an ''all you can eat'' policy. The smaller Sun Setting Room has a regular menu of fresh seafoods and steaks.

The veranda, as at any self-respecting summer resort, goes around the lodge, is decorated with window boxes filled with blooms, and has plenty of lounging chairs for guests to relax in and watch the sea. The large lawn stretches all the way to the National Park, where guests can swim and sunbathe on the sandy beaches. A number of recreational activities at the lodge include boating, tennis on Har-tru courts, deep-sea fishing, and golf as well as traditional resort lawn games like horseshoes and croquet. The lodge also provides small rowboats and sailboats for guests' pleasure. This is a fine old resort underneath a somewhat modern veneer, and offers scenery, fun, and relaxation.

Accommodations: 48 rooms, 31 in the old lodge; the 17 in the motel have private baths. *Driving Instructions:* The lodge is 14 miles north of Charlottetown via Routes 2 and 25. It is adjacent to the National Park.

LEA'S FARM TOURIST HOME

Vernon River, Prince Edward Island COA 2EO, Canada. 902-651-2501. *Innkeepers:* Ralph and Dora Lea. Open all year.

Most of the character of Prince Edward Island is found in the small rural communities and on the farms that dot the countryside. The Leas' large farm home has a kindly watch dog, big farm kitchen, and five bedrooms sharing two hall bathrooms. Ralph and Dora like nothing better than to share their house with friends and soon-to-be friends. The Leas raise beef cattle and ducks on their "honest-to-goodness" farm in a relaxing 25-acre setting with shade trees, an expanse of lawn, and swings for kids and adults. Guests are welcome to stroll about and look into barns and outbuildings to observe the farm operation.

This farm–guest house attracts guests from far and wide. Satisfied customers return again and again to enjoy the quiet and, most of all, the Leas' home-cooking. Meals are made from scratch in the farm kitchen and are served family-style in the dining room. Dinners (offered by request only to guests) are put on the table at 5 P.M. sharp. The menu varies each day and may include a Swiss steak, roast chicken, fresh fish in season, chops, or roast beef. With dinner are garden-fresh vegetables in season, home-baked rolls, biscuits, and pies, and puddings. Guests may choose between the "stick to your ribs" farm breakfast and the lighter "city slicker type" meal. There are many possibilities for daytime activities. All of the island's attractions can be reached by a half-hour drive or less. The provincial park's sandy beaches are twenty minutes away. Fishing is excellent in the area, and licenses can be obtained at the Vernon Co-op. The Leas will be glad to suggest island recreation and sightseeing favorites.

Accommodations: 5 rooms sharing 2 hall baths. *Pets:* Not permitted. *Driving Instructions:* The farm is 17 miles east of Charlottetown via Route 1, then Route 6, then Route 216. It is also 20 miles from the Wood Islands Ferry.

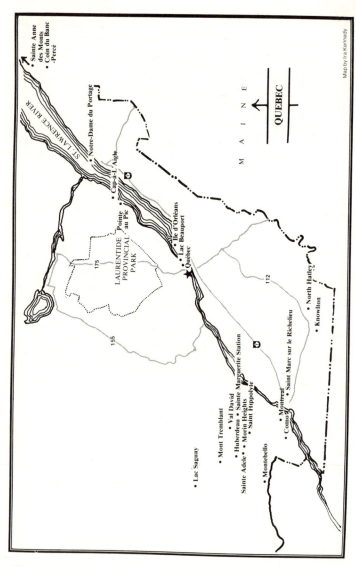

Map by Ira Kennedy

QUEBEC

MAINE

ST. LAWRENCE RIVER

Sainte Anne des Monts
Coin du Banc-Percé

Notre-Dame du Portage

Cap-à-l'Aigle

Pointe au Pic

Île d'Orléans

Lac Beauport

Québec

LAURENTIDE PROVINCIAL PARK

175

155

112

North Hatley

Knowlton

Saint Marc sur le Richelieu

Sainte Marguerite Station

Saint Hippolyte

Morin Heights

Huberdeau

Val David

Sainte Adèle

Mont Tremblant

Lac Saguay

Como

Montréal

Montebello

Quebec

Cap-à-l'Aigle

AUBERGE DES PEUPLIERS
  381 rue Saint Raphaël, Cap-à-l'Aigle, Quebec GOT 1BO, Canada.
  418-665-2519. *Innkeeper:* Ferdinand Tremblay. Open all year.

L'Auberge des Peupliers is more than 150 years old. So that there be no question of that, the 92-year-old *grand-père* insisted that we crawl through the bushes and under the house to see the hand-hewn beams that form its underpinnings. Chatting happily in French that largely passed our untutored ears, he pointed out the hand-cut joints and pegged timbers. Back upstairs, the family told us the history of the inn. Originally opened by Henri Tremblay, the father of the current proprietor, it operated as an inn in summer for thirty-five years until his death. It then closed for four years while Ferdinand Tremblay fully renovated the building so that it could operate all year.

  This is as Quebecois an inn as you are likely to find. The name Tremblay is as common throughout the province as the name Smith or Jones might be in an English village, and the inn fully reflects the family's deep-rooted French-Canadian heritage. You enter the building from its front porch into a narrow, low-ceilinged hallway from which a stairway winds up to the second floor. To the left is a sitting room with windows overlooking the Saint Lawrence. Old braided rugs partly cover the painted red floor. Handwoven fabrics

from the province cover the pillows on the wicker furniture, and an ancient family piano sits in one corner.

Upstairs are guest rooms furnished with iron or painted Victorian beds, handwoven bedspreads, and early chests, all tucked into the angles and dormers of the old farmhouse. One can come down a narrow back stairway into the inn's kitchen done in blues and whites: its color scheme is echoed by the adjoining dining room, where old oak chairs, painted or left natural, surround tables set with bouquets of fresh wildflowers. The dining room carries a three-*fourchette* (three-forks) rating by the Quebec Department of Tourism and features a selection of provincial dishes. The Tremblays are proud of their homemade jams, which are offered with breakfast every morning. In the back of the building is a recent two-story addition housing a small bar and lounge that is particularly popular with skiers in the winter. Works by local artists are displayed on the walls, and new French-Canadian pine furnishings are grouped around first- and second-floor fireplaces.

Accommodations: 8 rooms, 1 with private bath. *Pets:* Not permitted. *Driving Instructions:* Take Route 138 north of La Malbaie about 3 miles and take the marked turnoff to Cap à l'Aigle. The inn is on this road, the main street of the village.

AUBERGE LA PINSONNIÈRE

124 rue Saint Raphaël, Cap-à-l'Aigle, Quebec. GOT 1BO, Canada. 418-665-3272. *Innkeepers:* Janine and Jean Authier. Open all year.

A few years ago Jean Authier realized that his enthusiasm as a businessman in Montreal was rapidly dissipating. As he and Janine were driving along the Saint Lawrence north of Quebec City one day, he noticed an attractive home on a terraced hillside overlooking the river. In an instant and on the impulse of the moment, he went up to the door and asked the owner if he would consider selling the house. Naturally the owner was quite taken aback and answered that of course his house was not for sale. Undaunted, Jean made him an offer, and by the next day the bargain was sealed. The Authiers set out immediately to convert this house of recent construction into a comfortable country inn.

When we arrived, we were warmly greeted by Janine Authier, who showed us to her living room. The feeling here is very much of being in the Authiers' gracious home rather than in a commercial establishment. There are formal touches, yet the room is homey. An over-stuffed couch faces the stone fireplace. A telescope is set up by the glass doors so guests can watch the busy river-boat traffic. We stepped through the doors onto the terrace, where we sat in the warm afternoon sun enjoying a cup of coffee. If you look over the edge of the steep terrace wall you can still see the stone foundation of a much earlier house. The present inn was built in 1950 on this foundation. Jean plans to construct a wine cave below to augment the bar and lounge already on that level. During the busy winter ski season, a French *chanteur* frequently appears there. As you look out from the terrace you can see the beginning of a trail through the cedars down to the river's edge. If you walk the trail you can see several of the eight varieties of finches, or *pinsons*, for which the inn is named.

Guest rooms come in a variety of shapes and sizes. Many are paneled in local woods, and several have river views. Many pieces of furniture and some of the fabrics in the rooms are made locally in the Charlevoix region. Janine's passion for growing things is reflected by plants in most guest rooms, window boxes with brightly blooming petunias, and tubs of flowers on stone pillars at the entranceway.

The inn's dining room is small enough to qualify as intimate and to ensure that each dish is individually prepared by the Authiers' capable chef. The meal is centered around a basic table d'hôte menu with several choices for each course. "Les Gourmandises" options of particularly special dishes add additional cost to the basic menu. Notable among the list of starters is a very delicate smoked trout, a fine selection of terrines de maison, and a special soupe au gourgane de Charlevoix (a soup made with a local green bean that turns brown when cooked). Regular entrees include goose, salmon in shallot sauce, crepes fruits de mer, poularde petite mariée, and veal scallops. We were fortunate to arrive during the late June smelt-run and had heaping plates of this specialty. Among the many French pastries offered, Saint Honoré cake is a particular delight.

Accommodations: 11 guest rooms sharing 4 baths. *Pets:* Not permitted. *Driving Instructions:* See *Auberge des Peupliers,* above.

Coin du Banc-Percé

AUBERGE LE COIN DU BANC

Route 132, Coin du Banc-Percé, Quebec, Canada. 418-645-2907.
Innkeeper: Sidney Maloney. Open all year.

The Auberge Le Coin du Banc ("the inn at the corner of the beach")
is aptly named. It is on a 7-mile crescent of shorefront overlooking the
Baie des Morues (Cod Bay) and out to the Gulf of Saint Lawrence in
the distance. The two-story shingle coastal farmhouse was built about
120 years ago by the Mabe family (originally known as the Mabilles),
who had immigrated to the Gaspé peninsula via Holland and New
York.

The inn is a fine old country house with a decidedly Gaspésian feeling. On the main floor is a lobby filled with family antiques, wool carpets, and Canadian paintings. Verandas and terraces overlook fields of daisies and purple vetch and on out to the sea. Two dining rooms serve Quebecois and Gaspésian specialties including lobster, salmon, halibut, cod tongues and cheeks, crab and cod fish in several presentations, as well as other products of the sea. A number of meat selections include ham with pineapple, veal liver, pork cutlet, and two steaks. The inn has a well-thought-out wine list with about fifty labels.

Guest rooms upstairs feature antique beds with handmade quilts. One can curl up in an old rocking chair at the window and gaze out on the tranquil scenes. Other accommodations include a chalet on the mountainside nearby, surrounded by trees far from the road. Two little chalets right on the shore have antiques in the bedrooms and living rooms. These cottages are insulated for winter and heated by fireplaces and wood-burning stoves. Any choice you make is bound to be fun. The staff is an interesting group of bilingual folks of Irish and French descent. They will gladly steer guests to the best beachcombing and agate-picking spots.

Accommodations: 6 inn rooms sharing 3 hall baths; 3 chalets. *Pets:* Not permitted. *Driving Instructions:* Take Route 132 some 35 miles south of Gaspé. The inn is 5 miles north of Percé.

Como

WILLOW PLACE

208 Main Road, Como, Quebec JOP 1AO, Canada. 514-458-4656. *Inkeeper:* James D. Ross. Open all year.

Early settlers in this area were struck by its similarity to the Lake Como region of Italy and so named the town. Today the lake is called Lake of Two Mountains, and the Willow Place Inn stands at its edge just a few hundred yards from the ferry across to the Oka Monastery on the opposite shore. The Willow, built about 1820 as the private home of George Malette, was bought soon thereafter by Françoise Desjardins, the only French-speaking member of the small community. Almost immediately the building became the center of the Patriote movement, and so much plotting went on within its walls that the owner was finally imprisoned in Montreal and charged with treason.

When Jim Ross, a former Olympic bobsledder, bought the place, he decided to restore the look of pre-Confederation Canada. The result is an elegant and at the same time rural country inn that we immediately fell in love with. Window boxes of petunias and hanging baskets of geraniums greet the visitor on arrival; lilacs and daisies flank the paths to the front porch. In the process of restoring the inn, Jim and manager Scott Willows have exposed many of the inn's hand-hewn beams, refinished its hardwood, and uncovered a host of fireplaces closed up for years. In the front hall hangs a striking brass and cranberry-glass chandelier. The dining room has a variety of antique tables, each different, laid with antique lace tablecloths. Around the tables is an eclectic collection of chairs, the most distinctive of which are an antique bishop's chair and two early Victorian carved chairs from the Orient.

Scott and the inn's chef, both trained at Fenton's Restaurant in Toronto, have developed menus that reflect the produce of the seasons and English-Continental specialties. An ambitious summer dinner menu begins with soups like oxtail with profiteroles or cream of leek with Stilton cheese. Appetizers include guacamole, shrimp quenelles, sauteed mushrooms, and smoked trout and salmon, and main dishes include several steaks, fillets of trout, supreme of chicken, lamb chops with deviled sauce, and sole Florentine. The restaurant's English theme is capped with offerings of fruit trifle or fruit and English biscuits among the six desserts. Lunches tend to be lighter, with sandwiches, quiche, salads, and three hot dishes that recently included fresh trout, entrecôte, and a chicken curry with traditional garnishes.

The inn's guest rooms are filled with painted country-Victorian furniture. Their dormered walls have tiny floral print papers running up the sloping ceilings of the eaves. Old-fashioned quilts cover the iron, brass, and sleigh beds. One room, often used by honeymooners, has a canopied four-poster. Outside, the inn's swimming pool extends the enjoyment of the lake's waters. A nice side trip is to take the ferry over to Oka to explore the town and buy some of the monastery's renowned cheese.

Accommodations: 13 rooms, 8 with private bath. *Pets:* Not permitted. *Driving Instructions:* From Montreal, take the Trans-Canada Highway west, and follow Route 40 to exit 26 at Route 342. Turn right at Bellevue Boulevard to the end, then turn left on Main Road to the inn.

Huberdeau

OTTER LAKE HAUS

Huberdeau (near Arundel), Quebec JOT 1GO Canada. 819-687-2767. *Innkeepers:* Aga and Fred Thiel. Open all year except November.

Otter Lake Haus developed from a 1918 farmhouse at the edge of island-dotted Otter lake. In 1927 Hans Ebermann converted the property to serve as an inn; in 1964 the Thiels' bought the property, thus maintaining its German ownership for more than half a century. In the years since its opening it has been enlarged to include an annex and a cottage.

The inn is simply and nicely decorated, comfortable, and in a beautiful setting. Downstairs there is a small bar, living room, a glassed-in side porch crammed with a variety of plants, and a dining room that seats about sixty. At the bar one frequently finds Fred dispensing drinks and wisdom in three languages (German, English, and French) to overnight guests and villagers alike. Keeping an eye on him is a mounted otter that was trapped in the surrounding Laurentians. Rooms on the first floor have varnished wainscoting that rises partway up the walls with plaster above. Stained boards on the ceilings create a Tudor effect.

When we were there the tourist season was not yet in full force, and Aga and her staff had prepared a dinner with a choice of a fish dish and schnitzel. We started with homemade tomato soup, followed by a fine schnitzel with fresh vegetables, and ended with German apple pancakes with ice cream and maple syrup. The summer à la carte menu includes starters of marinated herring, smoked salmon, and homemade soups, and such entrees as smoked pork loin, veal cordon bleu, veal meat loaf, and German sausages with sauerkraut.

Guest rooms on the second and third floors share hall baths. All the rooms are paneled with varnished wood wainscoting on walls and ceiling. Furnishings of simple oak and maple furniture include a double and a single bed in most rooms. Beds are covered with blue woven spreads, and French Canadian woven drapes pick up the colors of the spreads and carpeting.

The property slopes gently to the lake. After a swim we rowed across to the island, where we explored the footpaths that crisscrossed it and stretched out on the smooth rocks to enjoy the late afternoon sun. Although we did not try our luck, the lake has been stocked with lake trout. In winter there are more than 30 miles of cross-country skiing trails accessible from the door of the inn.

Accommodations: 20 rooms, 1 with private bath. *Pets:* Inquire in advance. *Driving Instructions:* Take Route 15 north from Montreal to Saint Jovite, then take Route 327 south to Arundel. There take Route 364 west to Huberdeau. Follow the signs to Otter Lake (Lac à la Loutre) and the inn.

Ile d'Orléans

MANOIR DE L'ANSE

22 Avenue du Quai, Sainte Pétronille, Ile d'Orléans, Quebec, GOA 4CO, Canada. *Innkeepers:* Cecile and René Lemieux. Open May through November.

We discovered the Manoir de l'Anse by a stroke of good fortune. We had just spent the night on the Ile d'Orléans at a disappointing place. Feeling somewhat dejected we decided to lift our spirits by touring the perimeter of this pastoral isle. When we reached its southwestern tip we turned a bend to discover a wonderful inn on a point of land projecting into the Saint Lawrence River. Just as we pulled up, a river freighter was emerging out of the mist behind the inn, and the effect was magical. To our delight we discovered that the inn was indeed open and receiving guests for meals and overnight stays.

We entered the gingerbread riverfront hotel with its minaret-like towers and descended immediately to the dining room with food firmly in our mind. The entire room is, in effect, a gallery of the works of one man, a German wood-carver by the name of Mack. He arrived in 1954, and when he left, the room was filled with heart-back pierced chairs, wall plaques, chandeliers, buffets, and sideboards all carved by his hand to show leaves, castles, hearts, flowers, and fleurs de lys. As you dine you can watch the river traffic through a wall of picture windows. The menu tends to be more classically French than Quebec-ois, with offerings like lobster Parisienne, fillet of salmon with spinach, duck à l'orange, filet mignon bordelaise, civet de lapin, and quail with grapes. Vegetable and salads are ordered separately, as are desserts from the several french pastries offered each day.

We went upstairs to meet the Lemieux family, who told us they and their staff had spent an entire year completely restoring the old hotel from top to bottom. They began by stripping 150 years of paint off all the wood down to the turnings on the balusters. They revealed inlaid hardwood floors, and stained and arched wood-trimmed doorways, replastered and repainted. The effort was monumental but the results are worth every bit of their energy. A bar-salon is open to the public; a lobby used by guests for relaxation, television, and board games has a particularly nice antique piano that is more than a century old.

Upstairs are guest rooms tucked into the building's eaves and towers. The spanking white rooms have refinished floors, antique furnishings, and quilts on the beds. Two dramatic tower rooms (411 and 412) conjure up memories of Rapunzel. For recreation at the inn there is an outdoor swimming pool with golf nearby. But the best recreation of all is simply to enjoy this island with its high meadows ablaze with spring flowers and tiny French towns with stone houses.

Accommodations: 24 rooms, 8 with private bath. *Pets:* Not permitted. *Driving Instructions:* The island is just minutes from Quebec City. Take Route 40 from Quebec to Route 138 and then across the suspension bridge by Montmorency Falls into Ile d'Orléans. Turn right at the lights onto the circumferential road and drive to Sainte Pétronille and the inn.

Knowlton

LAKETREE SKI LODGE

Old Stage Coach Road, Knowlton, Quebec. Mailing address: R.R. 2, Knowlton, Quebec JOE 1VO, Canada. 514-243-6604. *Innkeepers:* Fritz and Ursula Seebohm. Open for lodging, breakfast, and dinner Christmas to March 31; for bed and breakfast June through Labor Day.

Laketree Ski Lodge is on the Old Stage Coach Road, over which passengers traveled in the early nineteenth century to get to trains that would take them westward to the prairie provinces or to Boston. The lodge appears to be a dormered house from the stagecoach era. It is, in fact, of quite recent origin but was built in the French-Canadian-farmhouse style. The mahogany-stained clapboard building with contrasting white trim and shutters stands on a knoll overlooking a 6-acre farm pond. There is a small glassed-in entrance where skis are kept during the winter season. One side of the lodge has a long wooden sun deck framed in the summer with twenty large flower planters. Surrounding the lodge are the farm's 400 acres, which extend onto the north slopes of the Sutton Mountains, a particularly scenic part of the Appalachian Range. On the property are two private lakes with boats and rafts.

The focal point of the lodge's interior is the living room, with its fine views of Singer Mountain. One entire wall of the living room houses the thousand-book Seebohm family library. The dining room has a brick fireplace and an open barbecue. It is here that Mrs. Seebohm presents her candlelight dinners to guests at the inn. The Seebohms are devoted organic gardeners, and many of the inn's offerings were grown the summer before in their own garden and then carefully frozen. Soups are Mrs. Seebohm's particular forte, and she makes a different one each day. Some of her favorites are oxtail, spinach and leek, fish chowder, cream of corn, cream of squash, and barley vegetable. Every evening a single entree is served to all diners. Typical would be German braised beef rolls, roast leg of mutton, shish kebabs, Flemish carbonnade of beef, duck à l'orange, or Vienna schnitzel. Mrs. Seebohm has personally developed many of the vegetable dishes she serves (such as her zucchini and leek dish), and she prepares her own sauerkraut. Desserts continue the German theme with Black Forest cake and fruit streusselkuchen, two of her many favorites. Guests sit at one large table and are welcome to eat as much as they like.

Each guest room upstairs is different, with hand-painted furniture done by Mrs. Seebohm in the manner typical of Bavaria and Austria. Rooms are named for birds, and the colors of the room are the colors of the bird for which it was named: Goldfinch, Bluebird, Purple Martin, and so forth. Also in the rooms are a number of early Canadian pieces and a few antiques from the family collection. In addition to rooms in the main lodge, housing is available in several cottages on the property, rented by the week, month, or season.

Laketree Ski Lodge offers fine cross-country skiing on more than twenty trails that fan out from the lodge. Downhill skiers have access to seven ski areas in Quebec and nearby Vermont.

Accommodations: 10 rooms, 4 with private bath. *Pets:* Not permitted. *Driving Instructions:* Take Autoroute 10 from Montreal to Route 243 and drive south to Knowlton. Continue on Route 243 for 6 miles past town; turn right on Old Stage Coach Road and drive a mile to Laketree Lodge.

MANOIR ST. CASTIN

99 Chemin Le Tour du Lac, Lac Beauport, Quebec. Mailing address: C.P. 800, Lac Beauport, Quebec G0A 2C0, Canada. 418-849-4461. *Innkeeper:* Denys Cloutier. Open all year.

This is actually the third inn to stand on this spot overlooking Lac Beauport. The location just fifteen minutes from Quebec City ensured its popularity even in the 1850s when the first hostelry, the Hotel Bagaouette, frequently played host to officers quartered at the Citadel. Fires destroyed both the Bagaouette (in 1939) and its successor (in 1959). When most recently rebuilt, the inn incorporated many architectural elements from Canadian-Norman architecture, of which the tower near the main entrance is the most characteristic. Throughout the interior the builders sought to create a rustic atmosphere with the use of exposed large beams in many of the public rooms, open-hearth fireplaces, and pine paneling. The feeling is further enhanced by locally handcrafted furniture and moose and elk trophy heads peering down in several rooms.

The modern guest rooms have contemporary furnishings, are carpeted, and have individual heat, full bathrooms, telephones, and television. Some on the lakeside have their own balconies. Many guests come to the Manoir simply for its food, which has won the four-*fourchette* (four-forks) rating from the Quebec Department of Tourism. If you are eating lunch or dinner here, we suggest that you manage a look at the dessert trolley before ordering your main courses. If you do, you will certainly save room for one of the large array of pastries. The dinner menu is extensive and supervised by Chef Morizot, who has presided here for seventeen years. There are a number of standard Continental dishes, as well as such specialties as pheasant with blueberries and port, entrecôte Madagascar, filet en bouchette, fillet of sole stuffed with mussels, cod liver and mushrooms, poached sweetbreads en timbale, and tournedos Helder. In all, there are more than three-dozen offerings. Popular after either skiing or swimming are the inn's Swiss fondue and beef fondues served in the Bar Alpin and the informal dining room, Le St-Dunstan.

Activities at Manoir St. Castin during the summer months include swimming in the heated pool or in the lake, tennis on two courts,

badminton, and use of paddle boats, rowboats, canoes, and the putting green. Eighteen-hole golf is available a few minutes from the resort. In winter the Manoir ski area is at its doorstep. There are six lifts, groomed slopes, and a number of cross-country ski trails. Snow-making has been introduced to extend the season at both ends, and lighting allows skiing at night as well. Skating and indoor tennis are a short distance from the resort.

Accommodations: 48 rooms, 40 with private bath; 4 two-room family units with private bath. *Pets:* Not permitted. *Driving Instructions:* Take Route 40 to Route 73 North (following the signs to Chicoutimi. Take exit 157 to Lac Beauport and drive 5 miles to the inn.

AUBERGE DU PAIN CHAUD

Lac Saguay, Quebec, Canada. 819-278-3226. *Innkeeper:* Henri Leduc. Open all year.

The Auberge du Pain Chaud is a handsome stone building with a second story of dark pine wood. Neat rows of windows are covered by striped awnings. The inn was built in 1947 on the shore of Lac Saguay in the heart of the Laurentian lake and river country northwest of Mont Tremblant, a Mecca for skiers from Montreal and upper New York State. The innkeeper, Henri Leduc, renovated the auberge in 1975, retaining its old-fashioned homey qualities. Its grounds are completely surrounded by a dense pine forest, with the lake off to one side. In warm weather, drinks are served on a terrace by the shore. The dining room offers a menu of Canadian specialties served with generous helpings of hot breads. Diners enjoy panoramic vistas of the mountains and lake the year round from this room with its warm colors and pine paneling, which is found throughout the auberge. The lobby and lounge feature big stone fireplaces where guests gather in winter after an outing of snowshoeing, cross-country skiing, or snowmobiling.

Guest rooms are furnished in a traditional early-1950s decor. Most contain sinks; four have private baths. The lake and environs provide year-round daily acitivities. In summer, Henri Leduc offers guests the use of rowboats and canoes for exploring the lake and fishing. There is a diving board for lake swimmers, and the shoreline is fun to explore at any time of the year. In winters one can snowshoe across or hike the woodland paths. On weekends at the inn there is dancing on the dance floor in the well-stocked bar, which also opens onto the lakeside.

Accommodations: 14 rooms, 4 with private bath. *Driving Instructions:* The auberge is on Route 117 north of Mont Tremblant.

Mont Tremblant

AUBERGE SAUVIGNON

Mont Tremblant, Quebec JOT 1ZO, Canada. 819-425-2658. *Inn-keepers:* Grant and Katie Moffat. Open November 15 to April 15 and May 15 to October 15.

We first discovered Auberge Sauvignon as we were winding our way down Mont Tremblant. Although we were there in early summer, we could well imagine its popularity with skiers—it is just seconds from the Laurentians' most famous slopes. The attractive stone-faced inn is just a short walk to Lac Tremblant and its waterfall. The river that feeds that falls runs just behind the inn.

The inn has a homey feeling. Its large living room has a fireplace and is a popular gathering spot in the winter, when guests spend quiet evenings reminiscing about the day's activities on the ski slopes. Upstairs are bedrooms, most of which share the hall bath.

Auberge Sauvignon is a true family operation. Grant does much of the cooking; Katie provides some of her specialties to the kitchen and generally acts as *aubergiste*. The Moffats' three children frequently help to serve the meals. The dining room has attractive formal settings on dark blue tablecloths. Meals are offered from the à la carte menu, with such starters as escargots with melted cheese, Grant's pâté maison of chicken livers, pork, and spices, coquilles Saint Jacques, onion soup (which they take three days to prepare in the classic manner), and Caesar salad. Stars of their entree menu include filet en chemise (a filet stuffed with pâté and topped with sauce bordelaise) steak sauvignon (a pepper steak flambéed at the table), chateaubriand, and roast rack of lamb, probably the most popular item offered. The most frequently requested dessert is the fraise sensuelles, in which the "sexy" strawberries are bathed in whipped farm-fresh cream enriched with Grand Marnier and served in a champagne glass.

Accommodations: 8 rooms, 1 with private bath. *Pets:* Not permitted. *Driving Instructions:* From Montreal, take the Laurentian Autoroute 15 to Saint Jovite, then go 5 miles on Route 327 to the inn.

CHATEAU BEAUVALLON

Chemin Beauvallon, Mont Tremblant, Quebec. Mailing address: P.O. Box 138, Mont Tremblant, Quebec JOT 1ZO, Canada. 819-425-7275. *Innkeepers:* Judy and Alex Riddell. Open mid-December to Easter and May to October.

Chateau Beauvallon was built in 1942 as a lodge-annex to the famous Mont-Tremblant Lodge nearby. The Quebecois-style building retains its ski-lodge flavor with exposed beams, pine paneling, and its original "Canadien rustique" lounge furniture. When Judy and Alex Riddell bought the building, it had been last used as the headquarters of the Red Birds Ski Club, which produced many of the top ski racers from eastern Canada. Judy and Alex brought several years of restaurant and hotel experience from Montreal when they moved to Mont Tremblant. Although they added some modern touches, the lodge remains steeped in French-Canadian traditions.

One of the innkeepers' prize possessions is their collection of antique Quebecois needlepoint tapestries, on display in the lounge and in the simple, paneled upstairs guest rooms. In the rear of the inn is its small dining room, again with pine paneling and more tapestries setting its tone. It overlooks Lac Beauvallon and specializes in home-cooked food prepared by the owners. Among their specialties are roast lamb, roast beef, loin of pork, chicken à l'orange, and Hungarian goulash. A fresh salad is served daily. On the way to the lake we stopped to pick fresh strawberries growing wild on the lawn. These raspberries and blueberries, which also grow on the property, are often the basis for the inn's desserts. The inn maintains an honor bar for its guests.

Chateau Beauvallon has its own sandy beach at the edge of Lac Beauvallon. Off to one side grow cattails, and the clear water has been tested pure enough for drinking. The lake is stocked with trout and has an abundant natural supply of tadpoles. While we lounged at the water's edge, the Riddells' dog, Daisy, entertained us by swimming into the water, plunging her head beneath its surface, and returning proudly to our feet to deposit an uninjured but no doubt greatly alarmed giant tadpole. The lake has but four houses on its circumference and allows only canoeing, so its tranquility is unbroken by the sound of motors.

Accommodations: 12 rooms, 6 with private bath. *Driving Instructions:* Take Route 15-117 (the Laurentian Autoroute) north to Saint Jovite. Turn right at the traffic light on Route 327 and go approximately 6 miles. Turn right after Villa Bellevue (see the signs to the inn) and drive just under a mile to Chateau Beauvallon.

LE MANOIR PINOTEAU

Route 327, Mont Tremblant, Quebec JOT 1ZO, Canada. 819-425-2795 (toll-free in the United States: 800-343-6768). *Innkeeper:* Claude Deguire. Open December 15 to March 30 and June 15 to October 15.

Le Manoir Pinoteau combines a round-stone first floor with an upper level done in Tudor-Continental style. Built in 1921, it has had its ups and downs in recent years but had acquired new owners and been refurbished just before we arrived. Behind the main building are a number of cottages, a motel unit, and recently constructed condominiums, none of which we visited. The inn has a fine setting. You can stand at the edge of the stone wall bordering the front of the terrace and look down at the lake 50 or more feet below, then along most of its 10-mile length to the Laurentian Mountains disappearing in the distance. The lake is the focus of much of the inn's summer activities, which include canoeing, wind-surfing, sailing, water skiing, scuba diving, use of pedal boats, and cruises on the lake in the Manoir's boat, the *Kon Tiki*. All activities are available to guests at reasonable rates.

The Manoir is an easygoing place that is making an attempt to attract a younger group of guests. As we arrived, musicians were setting up in the Musicale Jazz Bar in the lower level, and a newly installed health-food bar was serving lunch. After a meal—herbed mushrooms, crudités, homemade soup, and a "health" submarine sandwich of asparagus, fois gras, and cheese—we had a tour of the building. Each of the public rooms has a rustic, homespun look with braided rugs, stone fireplaces, Quebecois tapestries, log stools in the bar, and green plants everywhere. In the inn's guest rooms, chalets, and condominiums are a total of twenty-one fireplaces, some adorned with moose heads.

Dinner at the Manoir offers a selection of classic French hors d'oeuvres and soups and a choice from about twenty main courses including lobster thermidor, trout with tarragon, pheasant stuffed with chestnuts, tournedos Rossini, steak Diane, and coq au vin. A number of salads and vegetables may be ordered separately; among several desserts offered regularly are such flaming sweets as cherries jubilee and crepes suzette, which must be ordered for at least two.

Accommodations: 76 rooms with private bath. *Pets:* Not permitted. *Driving Instructions:* From Montreal, take Laurentian Autoroute 15 to Saint Jovite and turn north onto Route 327, which runs directly into Mont Tremblant.

Montebello

LE CHATEAU MONTEBELLO

109 Notre-Dame, Montebello, Quebec JOV 1LO, Canada. 819-423-6341. *Innkeeper:* Stanley W. Ferguson. Open all year.

Who could resist the opportunity to stay in the largest log structure in the world? The Chateau Montebello, or ''Log Chateau'' as many call it, almost defies adjectives. It was built in 1930 on property that was once part of the great feudal seigniory of Bishop Laval of Quebec and, later, Louis Joseph Papineau, whose imposing manor house survives near the Chateau. The construction of the Log Chateau, its huge garage, and Cedar Hall were a major endeavor. In just four months these three buildings were raised from ground to roof to encompass a total volume of 4 million cubic feet. In order to accomplish this feat, it was necessary to build a special spur of the Canadian Pacific railway about three-quarters of a mile long in order to deliver the 1,200 carloads of supplies to the construction site. At the height of construction a work force of 3,500 men had to be housed and fed each day.

The Log Chateau has a high stone-and-concrete basement, above which the main dining room, the grand ballroom, and four guest wings are arranged like spokes off the hub of the Chateau, the rotunda. As you enter the rotunda, you are transfixed by the central stone-and-marble fireplace, as large as a castle tower, rising to the cathedral ceiling many feet above. Fires glow in the six hearths of its hexagonal base.

Dining at the Log Chateau captures the feeling of eating at a baronial castle. The room is galleried on all sides, its ceiling the log roof far above. Ladderback chairs are drawn up to the dining tables; lighting is provided by lantern-style lamps mounted on the many stone pillars that support the gallery. There is a basic table d'hôte menu, with several specialties adding additional tariffs. Among the basic starters is an assortment of canapés, split-pea soup, spinach turnover, and sherried consommé. Regular entrees include salmon steak, breast of chicken velouté, beef Stroganoff, and veal scallops. Those splurging might try smoked Gaspé salmon as a starter or one of the sirloin steaks as an entree.

Guest rooms at the Chateau are less rustic than one might imagine. The log interior has been finished in a board-and-plaster Tudor style, with modern hotel furnishings. As a full-service Canadian Pacific resort hotel, the Chateau offers golfing on its eighteen-hole course, putting greens, tennis, swimming in indoor and outdoor pools, riding, shooting skeet, and trapshooting. In winter there is cross-country skiing, skating, tobogganing, and curling as well as sleigh rides. A sauna operates all year and the Chateau is filled with hunters during the fall hunting season.

Accommodations: 198 rooms with private bath. *Pets:* Not permitted. *Driving Instructions:* Take Route 40 west from Montreal to Hawkesbury, cross the Ottowa River to Route 148, and drive west to Montebello.

Montreal

ARMOR TOURIST LODGE

151 rue Sherbrooke, Montreal, Quebec H2X 1C7, Canada.
514-285-0894. *Innkeeper:* Morvan Annick. Open all year.

Armor Tourist Lodge is at the corner of rue Sherbrooke and DeBullion. The area contains a great many of Montreal's most fashionable shops and is central to the city's historic districts and McGill University on the hill. The lodge, at one time a fine Victorian townhouse, was built at the turn of the century. Its corner rooms are in an old tower, and other rooms open onto little iron balconies. As with many townhouses of the period, the lodge's first-floor entrance-way is a good half-story above street level and has wide stone stairs leading up to it. Good examples of the interior's fine woodwork may be seen in the foyer. Some of the guest rooms also feature the interesting wooden trim. Rooms here are simple and neat with large bay windows.

The lodge serves no meals but is just minutes away from many of Montreal's renowned eating establishments. Armor is a good alternative to the large, anonymous modern hotels and motor courts that dot the city and its outskirts.

Accommodations: 15 rooms, 5 with private bath. *Pets:* Not permitted. *Driving Instructions:* The lodge is on the corner of Sherbrooke and DeBullion between Saint Laurence and Saint Denis. The way to Sherbrooke is well marked, as it is a main thoroughfare.

CHATEAU VERSAILLES HOTEL

1659 Sherbrooke Ouest, Montreal, Quebec H3H 1E3, Canada. 514-933-3611 (toll-free from Ontario, Quebec, and the maritimes: 800-361-7169). *Innkeepers:* André and Marie Louise Villeneuve. Open all year.

For years, if a visitor to this city wanted to stay amid the splendor of old-fashioned Montreal his only choice was to book into the likes of the Ritz Carleton, gigantic by our standards. Recognizing the need for a first-class, European-style small hotel, the Villeneuves bought first one and finally a total of four adjoining townhouses in a fashionable district of Sherbrooke Ouest, near the Montreal Seminary and the Parc de Montreal. It took them a total of eighteen years to assemble and renovate the buildings with the dedication of true restorationists. The result is a hotel without peer in the entire city.

Probably the most impressive parts of the restoration are the extraordinary fireplaces in many of the guest rooms. Ours had a floor-to-ceiling mirrored oak mantel; the mouth of the fireplace was bordered with gold on white imported tiles. Others are marble, and some have elaborate moldings and miniature pedestaled shelves; each is a masterpiece. When we had finished gazing at the fireplace we could hardly keep our eyes off the ceilings. Most restorers would have been content to leave the high ceilings plain, as they found them. The Villeneuves insisted on reproducing a multitude of traditional encrusted cornices and medallions and then installing attractive brass chandeliers where many were missing. They fitted compact, completely modern bathrooms into each room, which they then furnished with the highest quality new hotel furniture, adding color cable television sets as a gesture to the modern traveler.

Downstairs is the reception area where, in typical European fashion, either the Villeneuves or one of their efficient bilingual staff greet you, make certain you are comfortable, arrange dinner reservations, point you in the right direction for tours of the city, and generally take care of you in a personal way that one rarely finds in larger urban hotels. Also on this floor is a sitting room for guests' use and a small dining room where breakfast is available on an à la carte basis. One major bonus of staying at the Chateau Versailles is that parking is provided at a lot a short walk away. The hotel is two blocks from the Guy Street stop of Montreal's modern subway system, and within walking distance are dozens of fine French restaurants. A fine introduction to the immediate district is Crescent Street with its small boutiques and cafés.

Accommodations: 70 rooms with private bath. *Pets:* Not permitted. *Driving Instructions:* Sherbrooke, a major east-west road through Montreal, is labeled as Route 138 on many maps.

AUBERGE HOLLANDAISE

Route 329, Morin Heights, Quebec. Mailing address: R.R. 1, Morin Heights, Quebec JOR 1HO, Canada. 514-226-2009. Open all year.

For many years this country hotel was known as the Swiss Inn. A recent change in ownership has resulted in the new name Auberge Hollandaise, but its Swiss origins are still intact and evident. The inn's masterpiece is its central lounge, a testimony to Swiss wood-carver Walter Darrow. The ceiling is supported by several tree trunks carved to resemble vine-covered trees. The tables are large trunks also encrusted with carved vines. Two noteworthy chairs could have come right out of "Goldilocks and the Three Bears." Each has been carved from a single piece of wood; the arms are intertwining vines that reach up to the backs, which are carved with Swiss mountain scenes, flowers, and flags. There is a stone fireplace in one corner, and moose and deer heads decorate the walls. In another corner is a split-log bar with matching stools.

The inn's dining room overlooks a curve in the river just outside its windows. Checkered tablecloths cover tables surrounded by blue chairs with red cushions. The Continental menu features escargots and mushrooms as starters, with entrees that include veal in several schnitzel presentations faithful to both the inn's Swiss and "Hollandaise" heritage. Fresh fruits and homemade cakes are typical dessert offerings.

Half of the guest rooms upstairs face the river and the pine trees. Others look out over the hill and the highway. They are all bright, and the bathrooms are new. The inn is surrounded by piney woods and hills perfect for hiking and cross-country skiing. Miles of well-groomed trails start right at the back door and lead around a clear mountain lake. In warmer weather the lake and streams provide excellent swimming and boating opportunities.

Accommodations: 10 rooms, some with private bath. *Driving Instructions:* From Montreal, take Laurentian Autoroute 15 to Route 364 (Exit 58) in Saint Sauveur des Monts and travel west to Route 329 North, in Morin Heights.

North Hatley

HOVEY MANOR

P.O. Box 60, North Hatley, Quebec J0B 2C0, Canada. 819-842-2421. *Innkeepers:* Stephen and Jeffrey Stafford. Open all year.

At the turn of the century, Lake Massawippi and North Hatley were popular summer-resort areas among visitors from the southern United States. One such was Henry Atkinson from Atlanta, Georgia, the owner of Georgia Power. In keeping with his Southern heritage, Atkinson decided to build a summer estate on the shores of the lake in the form of a replica of George Washington's estate at Mount Vernon, Virginia. For many years thereafter, Atkinson would arrive each summer with his entourage by private train, complete with horses and carriages.

So faithful was Atkinson to traditional building techniques that many who enter the inn assume it is several centuries old. This is particularly true of the Tap Room with its 10,000-brick, colonial-style fireplace hung with an antique musket. It is the focus of the Saturday night barbecues where the inn's chefs prepare charcoal-broiled steaks, fresh salmon, and live lobster at the hearth. The inn's main dining room is somewhat more formal with its linen service and the warmth of its pumpkin-pine walls. Here dishes like sirloin steak au poivre in champagne, tournedos Rossini, fillet of doré, and frogs' legs Provençale follow such starters as terrine de fois gras, hearts of palm vinaigrette, smoked Gaspé salmon, and lobster bisque.

After dinner, guests frequently gather in the sitting room, where cushioned chairs and a large braid rug are drawn up to the stone fireplace. If it seems that every room has a fireplace, it is almost true. In all, there are a dozen found in most public and several guest rooms. Throughout the rooms are the many fine Canadian antiques that have been part of the inn's collection for years.

Over the years the inn has grown to include not only the two main buildings but a number of smaller cottages. All guest rooms have private bath, eight have wood-burning fireplaces, and most have views of the lake. Colonial print papers and antique pieces set the tone for overnight accommodations.

With 1,000 feet of shorefront on Lake Massawippi, the water is the focus of activity. There is a safe beach where guests may swim, use pedal boats, canoes, and rowboats and fish for some of the lake's dozens of species. For reasonable fees guests may sail, water-ski, rent outboard motors, and take cocktail cruises on the lake. The inn has its own floodlit clay tennis court, and golfing is available nearby. In winter, guests may stay at Hovey Manor and use a special interchangeable ski ticket that is good at Mount Orford, Owl's Head, and Mount Sutton. When you arrive at the Manor, regardless of the season, you feel as if you are suddenly enveloped in a country gentleman's estate, surrounded by both creature comforts and magnificent scenery.

Accommodations: 34 rooms with private bath. *Pets:* In cottages only. *Driving Instructions:* From Montreal take Route 10 east to exit 121. Travel south on Route 55 to exit 29. Take Route 108 east to North Hatley.

Notre-Dame du Portage

AUBERGE DU PORTAGE
Notre-Dame du Portage, Cte. Rivière du Loup, Quebec GOL 1YO, Canada. 418-862-3601. *Innkeepers:* Claude and Ginette DeFoy. Open June 15 to September 15.

One of the most appealing hotels along the Saint Lawrence River, this Victorian summer resort looks for all the world like a large wedding cake. Its real character comes from its remaining relatively untouched by modern improvements, and many guests return here year after year. There are gingerbread balconies, verandas, formal flower gardens, and lawns going right up to the rock-strewn edge of the river. Old-fashioned lawn swings, rocking chairs, and wooden lawn furniture beckon weary travelers to come, sit a spell, and be lulled by the river's murmurings. Across the road are some motel units and a swimming pool that are part of the complex, with a mountain rising straight up behind. On the riverside are some attractive, old-fashioned additional cottages where guests can stay for longer periods.

Inside the big auberge one is struck by the timeless atmosphere. Turn-of-the-century wallpapers grace the walls of the two main salons. The riverside salon is furnished with wicker and woven-rush couches and chairs. The fireplace is constructed of beach stones. Quebecois needlepoint, famous throughout the province, decorates the walls. The mountainside salon contains many 1940s-style leather-cushioned chairs; card games are usually going at the games tables.

The large dining room has banks of windows overlooking the river and its many rocky isles. The room is decorated in greens and golds with coordinated drapes and slipcovers in floral pattern. The room's focal point is a large sideboard topped by a grinning lion carved in wood. This piece displays the silver tea services and serving dishes. The menu specializes in French-Canadian cuisine and fresh local seafoods. The big buffets are also great favorites with the guests. All meals are available to hotel guests and the public.

Guest rooms, off long hallways painted white with Quebec-blue trim, are furnished simply with traditional summer resort furniture and have walls of blue wainscoting. Room 110 probably offers the best river view, and rooms 112 and 111 have balconies.

Downstairs, next to the dining room, is an intimate bar decorated with drapes of fishnetting and dark woods. A homemade sound-muffling system is on the ceiling, which is completely covered with egg cartons. The auberge offers many traditional resort games such as table tennis, shuffleboard, tennis, and saltwater bathing. The heated swimming pool is across the road, a lovely golf course is just up the road towards Rivière du Loup. And of course, there is the quiet of the grounds with their fragrant gardens. An interesting and scenic drive along the river to the southwest will bring one to Saint Jean Port Joli, home of the famous Quebecois wood-carvers. At the many shops lining the route, visitors may purchase and examine these wares.

Accommodations: 36 rooms, 22 with private bath. *Driving Instructions:* From Rivière du Loup take Route 20 or Road 132 southwest and exit at Notre-Dame du Portage.

Pointe au Pic

AUBERGE AU PETIT BERGER

1 Côte Bellevue, Pointe au Pic, Quebec. Mailing address: C.P. 398, Pointe au Pic, Quebec GOT 1MO, Canada. 418-665-4182. *Innkeeper:* Jacques Lemire. Open all year.

Au Petit Berger is on a steep mountainside overlooking La Malbaie (Murray Bay), the Laurentian Mountains, and the little town of Pointe au Pic. The silver roof of the old church glistens directly below. A long country lane leads down the mountain from the highway to the secluded inn, a neat, well-cared-for auberge. It was built in 1896 for an American by a local architect named Warren. The area has long been a popular resort for Americans, English, and French Canadians. The Petit Berger, with black mansard roofs, is painted white and accented by black shutters and red doors. A wraparound porch festooned with hanging flower-baskets affords views of the Saint Lawrence river and the inn's flower gardens. Out back is a barn that the Lemires are restoring.

The house itself has been restored and remodeled and has an appealing combination of antiques, attractive rustic paneling, and homespun fabrics. There are green plants everywhere. French doors open into the guest lounge with its diamond-glass windows. Woven Indian and Mexican tapestries and needlepoint cushions add dashes of color and interest to the decor. The lounge is quite modern and informal with gray velveteen upsholsterd couches and greenery.

The guest rooms are up a wood-paneled stairway hung with tapestries. The rooms are very attractively decorated; Room 2 has the best view. A balcony is off one side of the second floor, and a turreted tower is in the exact center of the house. Rooms share baths that retain the old-fashioned fixtures.

The dining room and its meals are the pride and joy of the auberge. The name of the inn is a clue to the house specialty—regional lamb. Meals are offered to guests and the public alike. The dining room has been decorated in the blue and white of Quebec. The white-clothed tables have bright blue cloth napkins, well-appointed table settings, and fresh flowers in season. Homespun blue curtains hang at multipaned windows, and the room's atmosphere is further enhanced by the stone fireplace at one end. The attractive adjoining bar also has a rough-stone hearth. The menu at Petit Berger features fine French-Canadian cuisine. Dinner might begin with moules marinière or cucumber in a light mustard sauce. The five soups offered include vichyssoise, fresh pea soup with herbs, or marmite du Petit Berger. Varied and imaginative entrees include a number of lamb dishes and at least seven or eight others, such as seafood dishes, crisp duck, chicken, steaks, and liver, all with sauces. Meals are accompanied by a choice from several garden-fresh vegetables and at least four kinds of potatoes, salads, and a choice of tart, cake, or fresh fruits.

Accommodations: 6 rooms sharing hall baths. *Driving Instructions:* The auberge is about 90 miles from Quebec City on Route 362. It is near La Malbaie in Pointe au Pic up the hill to the west of town.

AUBERGE LES SOURCES

8 rue des Pins, Pointe au Pic, Quebec GOT 1MO, Canada. 418-665-6952. *Innkeeper:* Mr. Damerlis. Open all year.

We first discovered Auberge les Sources on an afternoon outing while staying at nearby Manoir Richelieu. We were delighted with our find, a country inn that had just opened its doors for the first time a few weeks earlier. The white two-story shingle inn is on a large, quiet residential lot surrounded by lawns, trees, and flower gardens. An old orchard remains near the parking lot. Hanging pots of flowers greet you on the porch as you enter through wide diamond-pane French doors.

Built about fifty years ago, the inn was for many years a summer home in this popular resort town. Its current owners have winterized the building and now operate it during the ski season (Baldy Hill is nearby) as well as the rest of the year. Especially nice in the winter are the seven fireplaces throughout the building, all still in use. Most of the interior of this house is covered with its original wainscoting, much stained or left natural, although some has been painted. The living room has soft blue wainscoting and is furnished in a blend of decorator-modern furniture and Canadian antiques. There is a small bar done in bamboo motif just off the living room. The inn's three dining rooms have fireplaces. Although the restaurant was not yet in full swing when we were there, the owners confirmed recently that their plans to offer gourmet meals have since materialized with a strongly Continental menu centering around several steaks, salmon, scampi and other fresh local seafood, as well as classic French veal dishes.

The guest rooms upstairs are among the most attractive that we saw while touring in this province. Each has diamond-over-split-pane windows, the warm wood on walls and ceilings, soft carpeting on the floors, and an occasional wall done in contrasting calico prints. Each bed was covered with a thick, soft comforter in designs matching the print wallpapers. Room 6 has its own sitting room overlooking the bay; another has white wicker furniture with yellow floral fabrics. This inviting inn shows the owners' skill in decorating and their love of plants.

Accommodations: 10 rooms, 8 with private bath. *Pets:* Not permitted. *Driving Instructions:* Take Route 362 directly into Pointe au Pic. Turn right following the signs to Manoir Richelieu and watch for signs directing you to the Auberge.

MANOIR RICHELIEU

Pointe au Pic, Quebec GOT 1MO, Canada. *Off-season mailing:* Auberge des Gouverneurs, 2 Complex Desjardins, P.O. Box 96, Montreal, Quebec H5B 1B2, Canada. 418-665-3703 (toll free from Quebec, Ontario, and the Maritime Provinces: 800-463-2820). *Innkeeper:* G. Miron. Open late May to late September.

In its heyday liveried chauffeurs would draw up to the entrance of the Manoir Richelieu and deposit the very rich of the northeastern United States, who would enjoy the splendor of this cliffside palace overlooking the Saint Lawrence River. When this life-style became less fashionable it looked for a while as if the Manoir would perish along with the era it represented. Then the Quebec provincial government had the good judgment to buy the estate and turn over its manage-

ment to the highly capable Auberge des Gouverneurs hotel chain.

Perched some 700 feet above the Saint Lawrence, the Manoir is reminiscent of a European castle with dormers and turrets piercing its copper roof. The stone building was completed in 1929, just in time to escape the ravages of the Great Depression. Its terraced lawn descends to a terraced overlook guarded by cannons, a further reminder of feudal Europe.

The main entrance is in the Manoir's lower level, where large stone columns support the enormous building above. Shops line the perimeter of the lower level, and a wide, sweeping staircase ascends to the Grand Salon. Two rows of columns flank this great hall with its upholstered chairs, polished brass accessories, and elegant green-and-pink carpet. Fresh flowers are everywhere, and at the far end a grand white fireplace proudly displays the crest of the Richelieus. Off the main salon is the main dining room offering French and Continental cuisine, a glassed-in Terrace Dining room, several smaller guest salons, and boutiques. Polished brass elevators conduct guests to their rooms above. There are also four six-bedroom cottages. We were lucky enough to get a room in the tower overlooking the river, where we could sit at our desk tucked into its curve and write letters home while we enjoyed the panoramic view. The large rooms have been completely renovated with queen- and king-size beds, woven French-Canadian spreads and, best of all, the original tiled bathrooms that pamper you into feeling like a monarch yourself.

As a full-size resort the Manoir offers virtually every summer sport and activity on the premises or nearby. Many guests come just for the chance to play its eighteen-hole championship course, considered to be among the finest in North America. In addition to the main course there is an eighteen-hole, par-three putting green. Tennis is available on three artificial-surface courts and an Olympic-size swimming pool is next to the poolhouse on the grounds. Riding is available at stables nearby, and on the grounds are croquet, volleyball, and lawn bowling.

Accommodations: 300 rooms plus cottages, all with private bath. *Pets:* Not permitted. *Driving Instructions:* Take scenic Route 362 directly into Pointe au Pic and follow the signs to the Manoir.

First-time visitors to Quebec City are astounded by the remarkable collection of stone houses and public buildings that have survived from the seventeenth and eighteenth centuries. We, as former New Englanders, tend to count buildings that predate 1700 as old. However, because Quebec City was built largely of stone, many structures survived when their wooden counterparts to the south perished, victims of decay or fire.

Quebec is a city of splendid small hotels, perhaps best described as urban inns. The greatest concentration is within a block or so of the Jardin des Gouverneurs and the Terrasse Dufferin. The latter is a 1,400-foot-long walkway that hugs the cliff edge of Old Quebec, overlooking the lower Old City 180 feet below. For us, all of the pleasures of Quebec City are to be found within walking distance of these small hotels, and we leave the New City to conventions and businessmen. Be prepared to walk (or treat yourself to a horse-and-carriage ride). There are few available parking places other than in parking lots, so cars are best abandoned for the duration of your visit.

AUBERGE LA CHOUETTE

71 rue d'Auteuil, Quebec City, P.Q. G1R 4C3, Canada. 418-694-0232. *Innkeeper:* Michel Poulin. Open all year.

The Auberge La Chouette is the only small hotel we list in Quebec City that would actually qualify in the strict sense of an inn, because it has both overnight accommodations and a restaurant. It is just across from the Parc de l'Esplanade, and one need only cross the rue d'Auteuil to book a horse and carriage ride or get up-to-the minute tourist information at the Tourist and Convention Bureau.

One enters La Chouette (the owl) to find a foyer in which the black and white tile of the floor is picked up by similar colors of the wallpapers and trim. A chandelier hangs from the ceiling, which has ornate plaster cornice work, characteristic of Quebec townhouses built around 1840. A curving staircase leads to the guest rooms above and to a now unused upstairs grand ballroom, a remnant of earlier days when girls from the Sisters of Ursuline convent school would sneak over to have secret dances with officers from the Citadel. The large guest rooms have brass, iron, or wooden beds and simple Quebecois furnishings. Each room is named for a work by Renoir, a

theme that is continued in the first-floor restaurant, which bears the artist's name.

On the restaurant's walls are small-print black, white, and pink papers; the windows have deep orange and rust draperies. Although a number of lower Old City restaurants, next to the Saint Lawrence, specialize in seafood, Renoir is one of the few upper Old City places that handle these dishes with expertise. More than a dozen offerings on its menu include spaghetti aux fruits de mer, darne de saumon moutarde, crevettes à la creole, sole amandine, and coquilles de crab Labrador. Meat lovers can order fillet of beef, rib steak Dijonaise, or fillet of veal Ile d'Orléans. The wine list at Renoir is more than merely extensive, with a number of fine château bottles and a total of 150 different labels presented in a 70-page binder. In addition to the more formal Renoir there is the Café Le Zinc. Decorated with a vintage-airplane motif, the coffeehouse has a copper bar and is a popular gathering spot for painters, actors, singers, and others interested in the arts of Quebec. Light meals including a number of special crepe dishes are served here daily.

Accommodations: 6 rooms with private bath. *Pets:* Not permitted. *Driving Instructions:* See *Manoir d'Auteuil*, below.

CHATEAU DE LA TERRASSE

6 Terrasse Dufferin, Quebec City, P.Q. G1R 4N5, Canada. 418-694-9472. *Innkeeper:* Claude Detcheverry. Open all year.

Standing one door away from the U.S. Consulate is the Chateau de la Terrasse. Of all the small hotels we have selected from Quebec City, the Chateau certainly has the most imposing view. Just a few hundred feet from the Chateau Frontenac and overlooking the Saint Lawrence River from its vantage point on the Terrasse Dufferin, this hotel is in a quiet setting in a cul-de-sac. Just a few feet from its door is a toboggan slide, the only man-made slide of its type we have ever seen in the midst of a modern city. Inside, the most striking feature of the hotel is its liberal use of leaded glass above doors and windows. The third-floor guest rooms have doors opening onto balconies overlooking the river. An elaborate staircase leads to the upstairs bedrooms past an amusing potted plastic palm standing guard in a small sitting area on the landing just up from the ground floor. The rooms themselves are freshly painted and contain modern furniture; several are equipped with kitchenettes. Parking is available for all guests.

Accommodations: 18 rooms with private bath. *Pets:* Not permitted. *Driving Instructions:* Take rue Sainte Geneviève to the end, turn right, and pass one building to the hotel.

CHATEAU DE PIERRE

17 Avenue Sainte Geneviève, Quebec City, P.Q. G1R 4A8, Canada. 418-694-0429. *Innkeeper:* Lily Couturier. Open all year. The Chateau de Pierre was built in 1853 by the Dugans, a wealthy English family. Like many houses along this street, it has thick stone walls that provide at once deep window-seat areas and freedom from the few noises emanating from the street below. The feeling of the rest of the hotel is captured by the lobby with its gleaming white Ionic columns, crystal chandeliers, silk-covered love seats, and red flocked wallpaper. Even the radiator has been dignified with a layer of gilt. Over the lobby fireplace hang portraits of King Edward VII and his Queen Alexandra.

A staircase leading to the second and third floors has a newell post bearing a bronze finial topped with its original gas lamp. During the day the stairwell is illuminated by the stained-glass skylight above. Throughout the guest rooms, the Couturiers have assembled a collection of formal French-Canadian Victorian furniture. The walls have Victorian-style papers, and the ceilings have the original plaster medallions, cornice work, and chandeliers. The rooms and suites are all carpeted and air-conditioned, and each has a bath and distinctive personal touches. Room 7 opens onto its own private balcony and room 1, on the first floor, opens onto a private courtyard. The third-floor hall houses an ornately carved harmonica organ dating from the 1870s. A Continental breakfast is included in the room rate, and nearby parking can be arranged.

Accommodations: 15 rooms with private bath. *Pets:* Not permitted. *Driving Instructions:* Take the Grand Allée to Avenue Saint Denis to rue Sainte Geneviève.

AU CHATEAU FLEUR DE LYS

15 Avenue Sainte Geneviève, Quebec City, P.Q. G1R 4A8, Canada. 418-694-1884. Open all year.

The Chateau Fleur de Lys shares with the Chateau de Pierre and the Manoir Ste. Geneviève the distinction of having been awarded a ranking of three *fleurs de lys* by the Quebec department of tourism, a major achievement for a small establishment in a city that is competitive among its many hotels. Standing on the corner of Sainte Geneviève and LaPorte, the mansard-roofed stone building houses one of the most formally decorated of the Old City hotels. The building's style is by the French lobby, displayed with its imposing chandelier. The high ceilings have intricately molded cornices and the floors, luxurious carpeting. Of all its air-conditioned rooms, the two corner bay-window rooms overlooking the Jardin des Governeurs are our top recommendations. Room rates here include breakfast.

Accommodations: 15 rooms with private bath. *Pets:* Not permitted. *Driving Instructions:* The hotel is at the corner of LaPorte and Sainte Geneviève in the Old City.

CHATEAU FRONTENAC

1 Avenue des Carrières, Quebec City, P.Q. G1R 4P5, Canada. 418-692-3861. *Innkeeper:* Leopold Schmidt. Open all year.

With five hundred guest rooms, the Chateau Frontenac is wildly out of scale compared to most inns and hotels in this book. However, it seems inconceivable to discuss Quebec City and omit this grand dame of the Canadian Pacific Hotel chain. Built in 1892 to a design by New York architect Bruce Price, the Chateau has a classic French-castle type of courtyard. As one enters from Saint Louis Street one passes under a stone Cross of the Order of Malta. The stone is a relic of the Chateau Saint Louis, the seventeenth-century governor's palace that stood on this spot for about a hundred years following Champlain's initial settlement of the town.

The Chateau Frontenac is a fairy-tale turreted castle. One does not have to be a guest to enjoy its splendor. Pause briefly in the courtyard and then explore the hotel's lower level, which has been transformed into Le Village, a series of little shops off a central cobblestoned arcade. We filled a bag with breads, cheeses, and sweets from the shops and then sat outside on a park bench on the Terrasse Dufferin and enjoyed both the view of the city and river below and our sampler of French-Canadian cuisine. For those with heartier appetites the Chateau has a formal restaurant known as Le Champlain (gourmet dinners with candlelight and soft music) and Le Café Canadien, which offers many regional specialties in a less formal setting. If you are to have one splurge in a grand hotel of Canada, our recommendation is to do it here or at the Empress in Victoria. In both, the grandeur of the nineteenth century lives once again.

Accommodations: 500 rooms with private bath. *Driving Instructions:* The hotel is on rue des Carrières, bounded by the Terrasse Dufferin, Avenue Saint-Louis and Avenue Mont-Carmel.

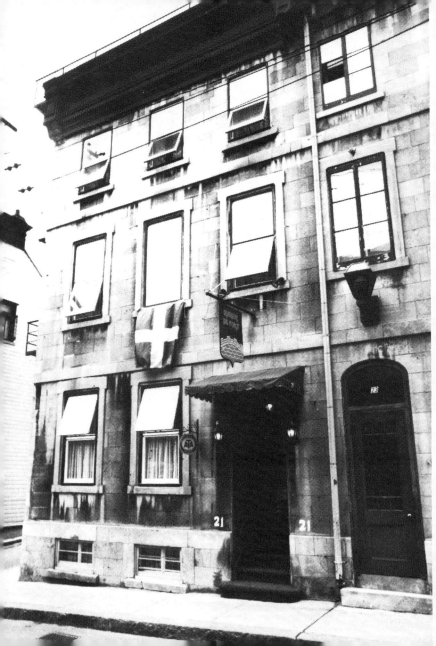

LA MAISON DU FORT

21 Avenue Sainte Geneviève, Quebec City, P.Q. G1R 4B1, Canada. 418-647-9357. *Innkeeper:* Charles Edouard Gagnon. Open all year.

La Maison du Fort was built in 1810 by Thomas Baillargé, considered the father of Palladian architecture in Canada, who designed the basilica in Quebec City and numerous other churches in the province. Baillargé's work can be identified by his use of sculptured rosebuds on windows and door frames. The Maison du Fort has walls up to 3 feet thick at the ground floor, and its roof is considered a masterpiece of construction—no nails were used in assembling the roof frame. In the course of its long history the house has been occupied by members of English society, including officers from the Citadel and later the bourgeoisie of Quebec. At one time the prime minister of Quebec lived here.

The Maison's engaging innkeeper, Charles Gagnon, bought the building (and one next door that awaits restoration) and spent all of the winter of 1978-79 restoring each of its eleven rooms. In some cases this meant the removal of as many as fourteen layers of wallpaper. Some rooms have oak and walnut fireplaces that were originally imported from England and, in some cases, are now equipped with gas grills. Windows are flanked by fluted columns and the walls have eighteenth-century-design wallpapers. The furniture is unpretentious but comfortable. There is a decidedly French feeling here; the paintings throughout the hotel have all been imported from Paris. At the time we were there, no meals were served, but Monsieur Gagnon was planning to offer breakfast in the near future.

Accommodations: 11 rooms, 7 with private bath. *Pets:* Not permitted. *Driving Instructions:* See *Chateau de Pierre.*

MAISON MARIE ROLLET

81 rue Sainte Anne, Quebec City, P.Q. G1R 3X4, Canada. 418-694-9271. *Innkeeper:* Fernand Blouin. Open all year.

Facing the city hall, the Maison Marie Rollet was built in 1874 by the Ursuline Sisters on land given to them in 1654 by the governor of Aillebourg. The first floor of the small hotel is the most handsome, with dark paneling, a fireplace, and stained glass. Unlike most hotels in the Old City, the Maison Marie Rollet has a small laundry area for its guests, handy if you plan a longer stay. The rooms are generally somewhat simply furnished; two have fireplaces that can be used. There is a third-floor terrace, or sun deck, that overlooks the gardens of the Sainte Ursuline convent school. No meals are served at the Maison.

Accommodations: 12 rooms with private bath. *Pets:* Not permitted. *Driving Instructions:* Take rue d'Auteuil to rue Sainte Anne. The hotel is at the corner of Sainte Anne and Avenue Chauveau.

MANOIR D'AUTEUIL

49 rue d'Auteuil, Quebec City, P.Q. G1R 4C2, Canada. 418-694-1173. *Innkeeper:* Jean Larochelle. Open all year.

Facing the Parc de l'Esplanade—where the horse and cariages park when they are not taking tourists through the city—the Manoir d'Auteuil is in a stone building dating from 1830. One enters an attractive lobby that sets the tone for the entire hotel. To the right is a large door with split, center-matched mahogany panels forming a large diamond pattern. Throughout the building the decor is an interesting blend of early antique pieces and the vibrance of an Art Deco remodeling that probably took place in the 1920s. Nowhere does the Art Deco state itself so grandly as in the hotel's bathrooms. If for no other reason, they would be a reason to stay here. Each is tiled and has rich blue and purple fixtures that could easily be in a museum devoted to the period. One bathroom is a full 15 by 20 feet and is reached up a stairway within its guest room. A seven-jet shower relieves weary travelers' aches and pains. We saw many of the hotel's rooms, and each was outstanding and different from the others. Some had carved oak or walnut antique furniture, while others had traditional hotel furnishings; all had thick, soft carpeting. Perhaps for all these reasons, Manoir d'Auteuil is the only Quebec hotel listed in the Guide Michelin.

Accommodations: 17 rooms, 10 with private bath. *Pets:* Not permitted. *Driving Instructions:* Take the Grand Allée to rue d'Auteuil.

MANOIR STE. GENEVIÈVE

13 Avenue Sainte Geneviève, Quebec City, P.Q. G1R 4A7, Canada. 418-694-1666. *Innkeeper:* Mary Coniveau. Open all year. Three of our favorite Quebec City inns are lined up in a row on the Avenue Sainte Geneviève (numbers 13, 15, and 17). Although each offers superb accommodations in a beautiful setting, it must be admitted that the view from the street-front guest rooms at the Manoir Ste. Geneviève is among the best in the city. From any of these rooms, one looks across the Jardin des Governeurs to the Chateau Frontenac in the distance. While we were there a flute concert was being given in the afternoon; in the evening the fog crept over the park, and one could hear horses clip-clopping as they pulled their carriages along the nearby streets.

The Manoir is entered through an ornate leaded-glass door to a small hallway that leads to the innkeeper's sitting room and kitchen. The central stairs lead to the guest rooms on the floors above. Some of the second- and third-floor streetside guest rooms have bay windows, and others have window boxes. Petunia and alyssum plants were in full bloom in our room while we were there. Each room is furnished with Victorian furnishings including overstuffed chairs and velvet love seats. Lighting is provided by crystal or brass chandeliers and matching wall sconces. This formal setting is enhanced by the wallpapers that often depict French scenes. Room 4 has a carved white-marble fireplace with a blue-tiled hearth. The mouth of the fireplace, which is no longer used, is closed with a scrolly black iron grille. Each room has been fitted with a compact and very modern bathroom. Upstairs is a small private terrace accessible from a third-floor door.

Sometimes it is important to seek rooms that do not front on the street. Here, in this peaceful part of the city, the opposite would be our choice. We enjoyed opening our windows and listening to the French-language radio stations while watching the quiet activities of the street and park below.

Accommodations: 9 rooms with private bath. *Pets:* Not permitted. *Driving Instructions:* The hotel is in the Old City, near the Terrasse Dufferin, at the corner of the Avenue Sainte Geneviève and LaPorte.

Sainte Adele

AUBERGE SAINTE ADELE

417 Avenue du Cap, Sainte Adele, Quebec JOR 1LO, Canada. 514-229-2745. *Innkeepers:* Huguette and Jean Paul Besnier. Open all year.

We have often described an inn as being high on a hill overlooking one sight or another, but we think the driveway leading to the Auberge Ste. Adele is the steepest we have encountered. The Auberge, a welcome relief from the dozens of motels that have sprouted up in this part of the Laurentians, recently opened under the management of the Besniers. It is in the small 1927 house that they have completely renovated. Most of the houses we saw in our travels in the Quebec countryside had roofs painted red. Here the trim of the white clapboard house is red. A wide, closed-in porch spanning one side now serves as an art gallery. Huguette told us their restaurant's popularity has already caused them to make plans to convert the porch to additional seating.

As you enter the inn you are greeted by a bouquet of wilflowers in the entrance hall. Here and throughout, the wood trim is stained and varnished. Down the hall to the left is the inn's appealing dining room. Here the light woods of the floors, tables, and locally crafted chairs merge into the cinnamon, olive, and beige tones of the wallpapers. Many of these colors are picked up by bouquets of fresh flowers on every table. In winter a fireplace adds its warmth. The fine luncheon menu features regional specialties, such as cretons, smoked trout, quiche made with Oka cheese, and tourtière Gaspésienne. Dinner starters include one of several cream soups or perhaps a petite marmite, followed by any of fifteen entrées including salmon pâté, fillet of doré Quebecois, stuffed crepes with shrimp, a ragout of chicken with forcemeat dumplings, several steaks including entrecôte au poivre, medallions of pork flambéed, and veal cutlet with mushrooms. Dinner can conclude with one of several plates of Quebec cheeses or with a dessert characteristic of the province, such as a coupe au perles bleues (blueberry ice cream sundae), tarte au sucre, or an apple cake served with maple syrup.

The old-fashioned guest rooms upstairs have flowered wallpapers of predominately beige tones. Plans were being discussed when we were there for the construction of a twenty-room annex, which may alter somewhat the overall effect of the inn. To specify an old-fashioned room you might ask for "une chambre avec un décor viellot."

Accommodations: 6 rooms with private bath. *Pets:* Not permitted. *Driving Instructions:* Take the Laurentian Autoroute (Route 15) north from Montreal to the Sainte Adele exit. The inn is just above the main road in Sainte Adele (watch for the sign).

GITE DU MONT ALBERT

Gaspésian Park, Route 299, C.P. 1150, Sainte Anne des Monts, Quebec G0E 2G0, Canada. 418-763-2288. *Innkeeper:* Quebec provincial government. Open mid-June to Labor Day.

Cutting like a knife through the mountains of the inner Gaspé Peninsula, Route 299 runs from Sainte Anne des Monts on the Saint Lawrence to the Baie des Chaleurs to the south. About a third of the way is Le Gite du Mont Albert, the official inn of the Gaspésian Provincial Park. The rustic, wood-frame inn is the perfect place to make a base while exploring the interior of the peninsula, a wilderness area frequently overlooked by tourists drawn to the more famous coastline. The dining room is a warm country place with polished hardwood floors; ladderback chairs are drawn up to small tables laid with red and white tablecloths. Hurricane lamps hang from the natural-wood ceiling, and plaid curtains are drawn back at the room's many windows. An antique hutch displays choice pieces of early Gaspésian pottery.

Meals are offered from a modest menu that changes daily. A recent selection included ham maple-smoked in the inn's smokehouse (a house specialty), shrimp omelet, lobster, salmon steak, scallops, cod tongues, lamb cutlet, and tournedos Rossini. In season, the inn also smokes its own salmon. If you arrive at that time, don't miss it.

There are guest rooms on the upper two floors in the inn as well as seven old-fashioned cottages. These vary in size and have painted wood floors, wainscoting, exposed-beam ceilings, and stone fireplaces. Simple Canadian furniture is the rule in the cottages. Most rooms have fine views of Mont Albert, a major attraction in the park. Many guests plan to spend the day climbing the mountain, and the inn provides guides. Trips to the peak involve lectures on the many unique plants and flowers that are found along the trails. This popular inn turns away about 1,300 people every summer. Plan to book early in the winter for the following season.

Accommodations: 21 rooms, 7 with private bath. *Pets:* Not permitted. *Driving Instructions:* Take Route 299 directly to the park and the inn.

Saint Hippolyte

AUBERGE LA CHAUMINE

191 Boulevard Lac Morency, Saint Hippolyte, Quebec JOR 1PO, Canada. 514-563-2355. *Innkeepers:* Henriette and Louis Gauville. Open all year except April and November, when only the motel unit is open.

The Auberge La Chaumine is a secluded log cabin (we actually had a little trouble finding it) that fronts on clear Lac Morency. Constructed of logs and thick clapboarding, the inn was built near the end of the 1930s. We asked about its name but were told only that its name ''sounds gentle to the ear.'' At any rate, it does not have a thatched roof as our rudimentary knowledge of French had led us to believe. La Chaumine is a rustic Quebecois lodge with, as Henriette Gauville says, "un coeur français."

Overnight accommodations may be chosen from the simple rooms with painted double beds and hall bath in the main lodge, or from more modern motel accommodations on the hill behind the lodge. The latter have continued the property's Quebecois tradition of being put up in the typical *pièce sur pièce* construction described in detail in the discussion of Auberge Handfield. If the bridal suite in the main lodge is available, by all means take it. It has a canopy built onto a sloping dormered wall and is rustically romantic.

The dining room occupies the entire back of the inn, its picture windows overlooking the virtually untouched lake. The interior wall is covered with machine-cut "logs," and bent-wood chairs are drawn up to tables set with fresh flowers. Hanging baskets in almost every window brighten things even during the winter months. One may order dinner from a table d'hôte menu offering the likes of tarragon chicken, blanquette de veau, boeuf bourguignon, and grilled tournedos. More elaborate presentations are available on the "Rendez-vous des Connaisseurs" à la carte menu, which has such starters as smoked salmon, asparagus in fines herbes, and escargots. This menu goes on to Caesar salad, a selection of soups, and about two dozen specialties including rabbit in mustard sauce, veal medallions in cream, sweetbreads, lamb cutlets, duck flambé, and trout amandine. Both of these menus change for spring and summer, although some favorite dishes are carried all year.

Just off the dining room is a small bar with a stone fireplace. Downstairs a second bar, which becomes a discotheque on Saturday evenings, opens onto a flower-festooned terrace that overlooks the lake. In the summer there is swimming in the lake, canoeing, pedal boats, fishing for trout, hiking, and volleyball. In winter the many Laurentian ski areas are nearby, and there is local cross-country skiing.

Accommodations: 24 rooms, 12 with private bath (in the motel). *Pets:* Not permitted. *Driving Instructions:* From Montreal, take the Laurentian Autoroute (Route 15) north to Saint Jérôme and exit onto Route 117 north to Shawbridge. Turn right at the traffic lights (on the right of the hotel there) and follow this road toward Saint Hippolyte and Lac l'Achigan. La Chaumine is on the left at the beginning of Lac Morency.

L'AUBERGE HANDFIELD

Route 223, Saint Marc sur le Richelieu, Quebec JOL 2EO, Canada. 514-584-2226. *Innkeeper:* Conrad Handfield. Open all year.

L'Auberge Handfield is one of the province's premier small country inn–resorts. Standing at the edge of the Richelieu River, the inn is the product of thirty-five years of effort by amiable innkeeper Conrad Handfield to collect and preserve early French-Canadian cottages in conjunction with his acclaimed restaurant. Over the years the inn complex has grown to include a heated swimming pool, seven cottages, a small motel unit, a sugar cabin of some substance, and, most recently, the installation of a dinner theater on L'Escale, a former Saint Lawrence ferry-boat. All of this is set on acreage that has been the Handfield family farm for many years in a town that has been largely spared the commuter development of other riverside villages.

The main inn, now used as the restaurant, is a building that dates back at least 150 years. Its several dining rooms and bar combine cream-colored stuccoed arched walls, hand-hewn beams, mellow woods, and Quebecois furniture to create a classic French country inn. Even a more recent addition, La Grange, preserves the feeling of the last century with its display of old carpentry tools including planes, adzes, and two-man lumbering saws. Throughout the rooms are antique clocks, copper lamps, an iron caldron stacked with firewood beside a hearth, ships of carved wood, and upholstered sofas and easy chairs from the last century. Meals at the inn reflect Monsieur Handfield's passion for French-Canadian cooking. Here one can sample soupe aux pois à la Canadienne, omelet au lard, ragout de pattes, boulettes grand-mère, lapin sauté aux champignons, fèves au lard, tartelette au sucre, and other specialties of the province prepared in a kitchen supervised by Handfield, who is president of the Association of Hoteliers of Quebec and a member of La Chaîne des Rôtisseurs and other gastronomic societies.

Totally captivating are the old cottages that have been transformed into overnight accommodations. We stayed in a cottage room that was built two hundred years ago in the classic "pièce sur pièce" style with thick slab boards laid horizontally to form the outer walls. The boards are exposed in the room's interior with the spaces showing

between them the stucco that covers the building's exterior. Also exposed are the original hand-hewn ceiling beams. Floors are carpeted, and modern baths have been added; but each piece of furniture is a gem of country Quebecois primitive design, their cracks and other flaws of age enhancing rather than detracting from their appearance.

A short walk down the river is L'Escale, where 550 theatergoers can have a before-dinner gourmet meal followed by a French-language play in a ship's large theater. Our French wasn't up to the task, but we enjoyed the experience anyway. During the sugar season (mid-March through April) the Handfield sugar shack is open to the public by reservation; visitors may enjoy classic French-Canadian meals in the cabin, watch maple syrup being made, and even book sleigh rides through the sugar bush. Just up the road from the inn is one of the many ferryboats that ply the Richelieu. We would take this one just for the ride—it even has its own birdhouse mounted on a pole, presumably for commuting robins.

Accommodations: 42 rooms, 31 with private bath. *Pets:* Not permitted. *Driving Instructions:* Take the Trans-Canada Highway (Route 20) from Montreal east to Route 47/223 (exit 112); drive north 5 miles on Route 47/223 to Saint Marc and the inn.

Sainte Marguerite Station

ALPINE INN

Sainte Marguerite Station, Quebec JOT 2VO, Canada. 514-229-3516. *Innkeeper:* Jacques LaRose. Open all year.

The best reason to visit the Alpine Inn is to enjoy its extraordinary log interior. Eighteen-inch peeled trees rise two stories to support the inn's cathedral ceiling. A grand staircase ascends to the second-floor dining area, where wrought iron and unusual pierced-tin chandeliers provide the lighting. Stenciling in the finest Swiss tradition is almost everywhere. Between the peeled logs in the ceiling are wide panels with the scrolly artwork. The edges of banisters and the backs of chairs share the art. Everywhere the warmth of natural wood is enhanced by the red wall-to-wall carpeting in both the downstairs lounge area and the dining room above. In the main salon are three large stone fireplaces.

The dining room is surrounded on three sides by picture windows overlooking the treetops and the river. Lunchtime each day at the Alpine offers a hot and cold buffet served on a long table upstairs. In the winter months the Sunday noon meal is an Italian buffet. The à la carte menu at dinner includes a fairly standard selection of steaks, lobster, scampi, frogs' legs, Dover sole, veal scallops, and steak au poivre. On Saturdays in the summer there is an evening "Gastronomic Buffet" highlighting fresh salmon, roast hip of beef, and lobster. Dessert specialties include crepes suzette, cherries jubilee, and pears with Pernod.

Guest rooms in the main lodge are intimate, with the warmth of horizontal wood paneling and plaid spreads on the contemporary beds. Most of the rooms have pine furniture crafted in Quebec. On the hill are a number of chalets. Winter activities include curling, cross-country skiing, and ice skating. In summer there is swimming in the heated pool, tennis, and golfing on the inn's private course.

Accommodations: 106 rooms, about 75 with private bath. *Driving Instructions:* Take the Laurentian Autoroute (Route 15) to exit 69, then drive east on Route 370 to the inn.

AUBERGE YVAN COUTU

Route 370, Sainte Marguerite Station, Quebec. Mailing address: P.O. Box 100, Sainte Marguerite Station, Quebec JOT 2KO, Canada. 514-228-2511 or 514-861-5212. Open all year.

Auberge Yvan Coutu is an old-fashioned year-round Laurentian resort reminiscent of similar sports-oriented resorts in New York State's Catskills. The Auberge faces Mont-Pentes ski area and is on 365 acres. Its facilities include the main lodge, built in Swiss-style in 1908, seven chalets, tennis courts, and a heated swimming pool. Everywhere in the main lodge are objects made of pine: chairs in the dining room are peeled-log construction with snowshoe webbing on the seats and backs; sofas and easy chairs repeat the basic theme with upholstered red-plaid cushions. Even the lamps and an occasional ashtray holder are made of twigs. The guest rooms are pine-paneled and contain local pine furniture. A guest lounge has dark carpeting, and stained wainscoting rises halfway up the wall to a plaster-and-board Tudor effect on the upper walls. Comfortable furniture is drawn up to the stone fireplace.

The dining room at Yvan Coutu has a table d'hôte menu that follows the same basic pattern each day, with minor changes from time to time and according to season. Typical regular entrees are boeuf bourguignon, salmon steak, chicken salad, steak au poivre, chateaubriand, filet mignon, and fillet of perch au Pernod.

The resort offers paddle boats, canoeing, archery, and skiing in the winter. Mont-Pentes has seven lifts from 300 to 1,850 feet in length covering fifteen trails.

Accommodations: 72 rooms, 16 with private bath. *Pets:* Not permitted. *Driving Instructions:* Take the Laurentian Autoroute (Route 15) to exit 69. Drive 4 miles east on Route 370 to the resort.

Val David

AUBERGE DU VIEUX FOYER

3167 Don Caster, Val David, Quebec JOT 2NO, Canada. 819-322-2689. *Innkeepers:* Jocelyn-Louis Hardy and Michel Giroux. Open all year.

This auberge is an attractive, relatively new (1959) Swiss-style chalet with two new additions. It is centrally located in the scenic Laurentians just across from the Mont-Plante ski area and next to its own lake. The area is laced with excellent cross-country trails; one of the best trail systems in the Laurentians leads directly from the inn's doorstep. The grounds around the inn are dotted with varieties of pines; in warm weather, flowers are everywhere, in true Swiss tradition. The two cousins who operate the inn provide warm personal attention to their guests. One is drawn immediately to the informal rustic living room. The focal point is a large stone fireplace that warms the sitting areas. On one side of the hearth is a dutch oven where the innkeepers bake bread each morning.

The auberge and Val David are favorites of many local artists and those from Montreal and New York areas. The benefits of this popularity are walls decorated with weavings and original artwork. The rooms are furnished with locally crafted pine. The pine-paneled dining room features round tables of 2-inch-thick pine, together with chairs fashioned from peeled logs. The inn's look and feel are Swiss and Quebecois. Specialties in the dining rom are the home-baked breads that accompany quiches, fondues, steaks, boeuf bourguignon, and coq au vin. Dessert favorites are chocolate fondues and apple and sugar pies.

For entertainment the innkeepers provide a bar and recreation room with billiards, table tennis, and television. There are a number of outdoor resort activities, such as badminton, and Val David's skiing facilities. This popular tourist village has such year-round attractions as boutiques, theater, outdoor concerts, and horseback riding.

Accommodations: 21 rooms, 6 with private bath, 15 sharing hall baths. *Pets:* Not permitted. *Driving Instructions:* Take Laurentian Autoroute (Route 15) exit 76 to Val David. The inn is 2 miles from the village, near Mont Plante.

AUBERGE LE RUCHER

2368 L'Eglise, Val David, Quebec JOT 2NO, Canada. 819-322-2507. *Innkeepers:* Luc and Florence Invernizzi. Open June 1 through the following Easter.

The Auberge Le Rucher was built over a five-year period by its owners, Luc and Florence Invernizzi, who set out to re-create a French alpine inn and clearly had fun in the process. Throughout the inn they left ceiling beams exposed and, in many places, covered the walls with stained wide boards. The clever use of new materials in traditional ways extends to guest rooms, where several beds have "four-poster" canopies supported by standard-dimension lumber draped with sheer material. This is very much an inn a friend of ours would call a "hidey-hole" place, with nooks and crannies and doors cut to fit the angles of the roofline. Where the Invernizzis did not make furniture, they fitted the rooms with Canadian pine antiques, rush-seat chairs, and locally woven spreads. Four of the rooms have

working fireplaces, and all but two have private baths, several of which Luc managed to fit under the eaves in amusing ways.

Dining on several levels includes a glassed-in terrace with stucco walls and an indoor room whose window wall overlooks the inn's indoor swimming pool. The menu of French dishes included quail, a favorite of ours. Luc told of an earlier time when the inn kept quail in a cage near the dining room for guests' amusement. However, many feared that the quail they saw on entering would finally end up on their plates, so Luc finally set them free. The Auberge le Rucher is one with "beaucoup des petits coins" (many little nooks); it is thoroughly French and lots of fun.

Accommodations: 14 rooms, 12 with private bath. *Driving Instructions:* Take Route 15 north to exit 76, then drive 5 miles on Route 117 to Val David. The inn is in the center of town.

LA SAPINIÈRE

Val David, Quebec JOT 2NO, Canada. 819-322-2020. *Innkeeper:* Marie Brancolini. Open all year.

If you were to ask any French Canadian to name the top five resorts in the province, it is almost certain that the name of La Sapinière would lead the list. La Sapinière ("the Firwood") has grown greatly from the original log cabin built by Mr. Dufresne's father as a way of keeping the men of his lumber company employed during the Depression. The original lodge has expanded time after time; there are now dozens of separate cottages and all the facilities of a major resort. Accommodations in the main building are modern, almost motel-like in feeling. Cottages range in size and number of bedrooms; several have their own living rooms and fireplaces. So comfortable are the accommodations and so thorough are the services offered to guests that the Ministry of Tourism awarded the resort a rating of five *fleurs de lys* indicating very good comfort and spaciousness.

Of even greater importance to us was the ministry's award of four *fourchettes* (four forks) to the kitchen at La Sapinière. In fact, the fame of executive chef Marcel Kretz had already reached our ears before we left home. Kretz has served as captain of Canada's team in the culinary Olympics and has won numerous awards for his cooking. It has always been the policy of the Dufresnes to give him a totally free hand with food purchasing. The result is that so much is spent on obtaining the very best ingredients that the kitchen rarely shows much of a profit, though its fine cuisine keeps the resort at or near capacity almost all year. Every day a menu is planned to capitalize on the ingredients at their peak at that moment. If Kretz has been able to gather some of his prized wild mushrooms, they will be featured in one or more dishes. The pâtés or terrines of the day are equally timely. Much of the smoked fish is prepared in the kitchen's own smokehouse. In salmon season a variety of presentations utilize this most prized Canadian fish, which is served only when available fresh. We had smoked trout and salmon mousse followed by a fine beef Wellington. At breakfast we sampled fèves au lard and cretons—the best we had in the province—from a long line of hot and cold offerings from the buffet. The dining room has large picture windows overlooking the lake.

After lunch we took out a canoe and explored the waterway feeding the lake; paddle boats were also available at the dock. We meandered past beaver dams, watched over by a variety of wild birds, and stayed out almost until dusk when the shadows played on the tall cliff in the distance. La Sapinière is the only Canadian resort that is a member of the distiguished Relais de Campagne, based in Europe.

Accommodations: 70 rooms with private bath. *Pets:* Not permitted. *Driving Instructions:* Take exit 76 from Route 15 and drive 2 miles on Route 117 to the Val David traffic lights. Turn right and drive a mile to La Sapinière.

PARKER'S LODGE
1340 Lac Paquin Road, Val David, Quebec JOT 2NO, Canada. 819-322-2026. *Innkeeper:* John B. Parker. Open all year.
The brochure said that the setting was magnficent, but we have been disappointed before. This was not to be the case at Parker's Lodge. A broad lawn sweeps down over several terraces to the lake, which disappears around a curve of maples and pines. Don't be disappointed when you first pull up. The lodge's best face is kept toward Lac Paquin, which provides many of the inn's summer activities, including swimming and boating. The latter is covered by the basic room rate. Other summer activities include barbecues on the patio and pic-

nics. In winter the lodge is populated by skiers drawn to the fine area slopes and cross-country trails.

Parker's Lodge dates from 1910, with additions and renovations over the years. The most recent resulted in the liberal use of pine paneling and the installation of broad sliding glass doors that overlook the lake. Hardwood floors have braided area rugs, and there is a blend of contemporary furniture and the Parker's antiques. Despite such modern touches as acoustical tile on the ceilings, Parker's remains a friendly, inviting place with lots of books and magazines that invite guests to relax and enjoy the lodge's setting.

Simple guest rooms on the upper two floors have picture windows overlooking the lake or the surrounding hills. All have the handwoven Quebecois bedspreads so popular in the province. Rooms range from double rooms with running water to a two-bedroom chalet with private bath and fireplace. John Parker takes the entertainment of his guests seriously. Most evenings he leads a sing-along in which his bartender plays the piano and he provides the rhythm section. He is also an old-movie devotee and has created a miniature movie theater with tiered rows of upholstered sofas for their better enjoyment. John also presides over the family-style meals, where guests sit around large oval antique tables to enjoy the inn's home-cooking. Quiches and fresh berry and fruit pies are specialties.

Accommodations: 18 rooms, 12 with private bath. *Driving Instructions:* The inn is on Lac Paquin Road, ¼ mile west of exit 50 on the Laurentian Autoroute (Route 15).

Index

THE COMPLEAT TRAVELER'S READER REPORT

To: *The Compleat Traveler*
    c/o Burt Franklin & Co., Inc.
    235 East 44th Street
    New York, New York 10017 U.S.A.

Dear Compleat Traveler:

I have used your book in _____ (country or region).
I would like to offer the following ☐ new recommendation, ☐ comment,
☐ suggestion, ☐ criticism, ☐ or complaint about:

Name of Country Inn or Hotel:

_____

Address: _____

_____

Comments:

Day of my visit: _____   Length of stay: _____

From (name): _____

Address _____

_____ Telephone: _____